I Am
That Child

Changing Hearts and Changing the World

Elizabeth Geitz

Morehouse Publishing
NEW YORK · HARRISBURG · DENVER

Unless otherwise noted, the Scripture quotations contained herein are from the New Revised Standard Version Bible, copyright © 1989 by the Division of Christian Education of the National Council of Churches of Christ in the U.S.A. Used by permission. All rights reserved.

A significant portion of the proceeds from the sale of this book will be used to fund self-sustaining projects of the Good Shepherd Home, Cameroon, West Africa.

I Am That Child is a work of non-fiction. However, the venue and timing of some conversations have been altered to aid the flow of the story, and the orphans' names have been changed to protect their identity.

Morehouse Publishing, 4775 Linglestown Road, Harrisburg, PA 17112

Morehouse Publishing, 445 Fifth Avenue, New York, NY 10016

Morehouse Publishing is an imprint of Church Publishing Incorporated.
www.churchpublishing.org

Cover art: "Morning Chores at the Good Shepherd Home," photograph by Elizabeth Geitz, 2008. Used with permission.

Photographs of the Home and Children by Elizabeth Geitz, 2008. Used with permission.

Cover design by Laurie Klein Westhafer

Library of Congress Cataloging-in-Publication Data

Geitz, Elizabeth Rankin.
I am that child : changing hearts and changing the world / Elizabeth Geitz.
    p. cm.
Includes bibliographical references.
ISBN 978-0-8192-2778-2 (pbk.)—ISBN 978-0-8192-2779-9 (ebook)   1. Geitz, Elizabeth Rankin. 2. Orphanages—Cameroon. 3. Orphans—Cameroon. 4. Church work with orphans—Cameroon. 5. Children—Cameroon—Social conditions. I. Title.
HV1359.5.G45 2012
362.73092—dc23
[B]
                              2011037876

Printed in the United States of America

10 9 8 7 6 5 4 3 2 1

Dedicated to Annie Livingston Harris and Anner Weakley,
whose unconditional love has sustained me throughout my life

Contents

Contents

PART IV / Lives Intertwined

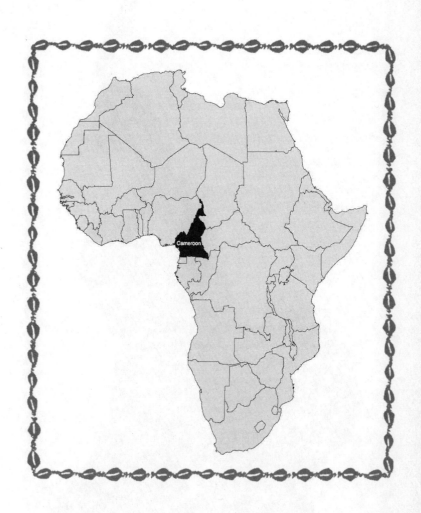

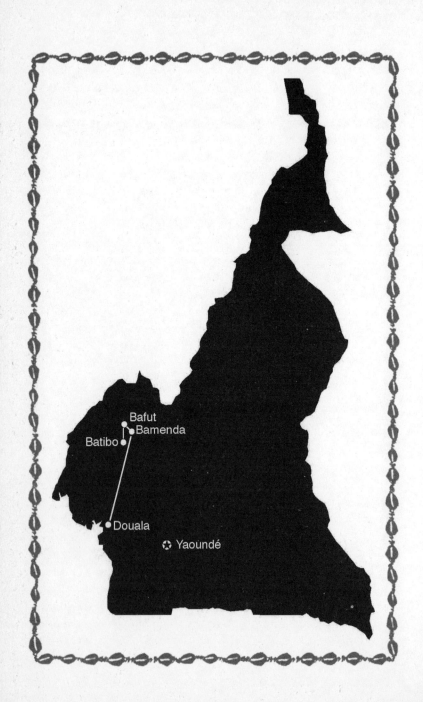

Bafut
Bamenda
Batibo
Douala
✪ Yaoundé

Introduction

At the end of a steep, deeply rutted dirt road
slick with rains of the season
lies the heart of Cameroon—
beating, beating, beating
into the night
early in the morning
cuddling, feeding, loving
the orphaned children of the Northwest Province.

Fifty thousand strong
they cry out
to be sheltered, fed, spirited away
from the ravages of villagers who don't care.
AIDS orphans, epileptic orphans
the work of witchcraft,
"Not in my house, not with my children.
There's no room at the inn for you and you and you."

The heart beats
the arms open wide
as Sister Jane Mankaa welcomes each one
as her own beloved child,
miraculously an orphan no more.

At the dawn of the new millennium, Jane Mankaa boarded a plane for America with a dream in her heart, a vision in her head, and $25 in her pocket.

Having never ventured far from the bush of Cameroon in West Africa, Jane boarded the plane filled with determination. She spent a year with a group of women in Iowa, where she felt called to become a nun and establish an orphanage in her country. She wrote letters to every Episcopal convent in the United States, and one responded affirmatively—the Community of St. John Baptist in Mendham, New Jersey.

After a transformative year in New Jersey, Sister Jane was ready to get started. When she returned to Africa, local women began to sit and learn from her. One by one they asked to join the Anglican Benedictine order she was establishing, and one by one she said "yes." With great care, she bargained for what would become the Good Shepherd Home Orphanage, and the women soon moved in with her. They prayed and worked together; in 2003 the first orphan arrived, then another, and another. Now there are 130 orphans that call Good Shepherd their home.

Was it a journey, a pilgrimage, or an adventure that my traveling companions and I made to the Good Shepherd Home? In July 2008 we joined the women who sat at Sister Jane's feet and we learned—about the orphans' lives, our own childhoods in the segregated South, and the bonds of affection that develop across cultural boundaries. After arriving home, I transcribed recordings of our conversations and then spent another two and a half years researching how Americans might partner with our African neighbors in a way that truly matters, because it is nothing less than a matter of life and death.

These children have the capacity to become Africa's leaders of tomorrow. May they change your heart as they have changed mine.

Most gracious and loving Creator,
be with the children of the Good Shepherd Home.
You know their needs before I ask:
Safety from thieves who roam the dark nights,
beds of their own,
rains for the harvest,
wood for the bakery,
food for the rabbits and pigs.

Thank you for their indomitable spirits,
their compassionate hearts,
their steadfast faith in you
to provide the food in their bellies,
the clothes on their backs,
the shelter over their heads,
through your hands and feet on earth.

Elizabeth Geitz
October 2011

PART I

The Road to Cameroon

"Life loves to be taken by the lapel and told, 'I'm with you kid, let's go.'"

—*Maya Angelou*

"I don't believe in charity. I believe in solidarity . . .
It respects the other and learns from the other. I have a lot to learn from other people."

—*Eduardo Galeano*

CHAPTER 1

Witchcraft and Southern Roots

Sister Jane is a born storyteller who highlights a story by lowering her voice, widening her eyes, or slapping her fist in the palm of her hand. Ebony skin against white nun's habit, face radiating joy, her presence never fails to fill a room. I saw it happen at a gathering in America, where she was sharing stories of the orphanage she had established several years earlier in Cameroon, West Africa.

"I was here in your country in 2003," she told us, "when I received an urgent e-mail from Sister Précis, one of the nuns at the orphanage. 'You've got to come back immediately!' it said. 'The other Sisters and I can no longer stay in this house. We are terrified. There are large snakes, witch snakes that disappear completely when we try to kill them. The work of the witch down the road. We cannot stay. We're leaving our dogs behind and getting out of here tonight. Hurry! We need you here!'"

"You know," she went on to explain, "only a witch snake can totally disappear like that. They are big, huge really. Something that big can't just disappear unless it's through witchcraft. So with all the Sisters gone from the home, I had to go back to solve the problem."

"When I got back to Cameroon, I brought friends to the house with me so I wouldn't have to enter alone," Sister Jane continued, brown eyes sparkling. "While they were examining every nook and cranny of that abandoned house, one of the dogs dug up a twelve-inch clay pot in the front yard. In it we found someone's hair, a small spear, a knife, coins, and a tiny bag with black stuff inside. All signs of witchcraft. Then the minister who had sold us the house came over. We gathered up all the things that had been buried in that pot and burned them. Afterward, we put the ashes on the road going to the man's house who we knew had done the witchcraft.

"When the man saw the ashes, there was no doubt in his mind as to what they were. 'Why'd ya put those ashes on my road?' he screamed the first time he saw me. 'Because you're the one doing the witchcraft!' I yelled back at him. The man did not defend himself. He just went home and two months later he moved out." As she finished her story, Sister Jane crossed her arms in front of her with a satisfied look on her face.

"Our spirit of prayer was disturbing him, and that house of his collapsed," she explained. "He only came back to sell it to us. So we bought it and completely destroyed it. And then we bought the property next to it. We got that, too and that's where the Good Shepherd Home is now."

Sister Jane was lost in thought. "We have not had it easy trying to establish our orphanage," she sighed. "No, we have not had it easy."

And this was just the beginning.

Sitting with me that morning were two women who were as captivated by Sister Jane as I was: Lillian Cochran, who had previously visited the orphanage, and Nan Curtis. Three years later, we took the unlikely leap of journeying to Africa together.

We had no idea what we would find when we arrived. One afternoon we saw each other in town and shared stories of our very different preparation procedures.

"I can't believe we leave in a month. I don't think it's sunk in yet," said Nan, a trim woman in her late forties with short brown hair.

"How about bug spray? Have you all bought any?" I asked, filled with last-minute questions. "They say there's a kind of malaria peculiar to Cameroon that's resistant to pills. I don't know what to do—cover my face with a net I guess, get a mosquito net for the bed, and douse myself with the best bug spray I can find."

"Elizabeth," said Lillian, a spry and bright woman in her eighties, "I've told you a hundred times that I never saw one mosquito when I visited the orphanage four years ago. Not one. Don't worry about it. You won't need any of that stuff."

"But my guide book says the type of malaria you can get in certain areas of Africa is awful and I'm not taking any chances," I responded.

Clearly we needed to do a more thorough review, so we set a wine and cheese date at my house exactly two weeks before departure. Nan arrived with the three donated laptops we were taking in our carry-on luggage for the children. Then Lillian joined us. Sitting on my couch that was covered in cream-colored silk, our plate of cheese on a tea table in front of us, I could see the stark contrast between our lives here and the community we would soon be visiting.

"Why did you all decide to do this?" I asked. I'd been wrestling with my own motivations and was curious about theirs. We hadn't known each other well prior to this. We were church friends who occasionally had dinner in one another's homes, but not much more. We were all concerned about helping our neighbors both near and far. But why Africa? Why now? And why the three of us?

"There are a lot of different factors for me," I volunteered. "Certainly part of it is the work I did with African Americans twenty years ago in the inner city. While I was there I felt called to become an Episcopal priest. Now that I've been ordained fifteen years, I've been given a sabbatical and initially had no idea how to spend it. Then I suddenly remembered something. In the late seventies, I was watching *The Today Show* with my husband when Miz Lillian Carter was being interviewed; she began relating a mesmerizing story about her visit to an African village. Suddenly there was a picture of her sitting on a motorcycle with a big smile on her face, surrounded by about thirty village children. 'That's going to be me someday, minus the motorcycle,' I told my husband, filled with conviction. But the biggest factor for me by far was meeting Sister Jane three years ago. Her deep sense of spirituality and ability to communicate the love of God never fails to draw me to her. Not to mention her determination and perseverance."

"I know," said Lillian, nodding her head. "She's the reason I decided to visit her orphanage four years ago and why I started a sponsorship program for the children when I returned."

As soon as I heard about the program, I immediately signed up to sponsor five-year-old Nafi Ndika. I had wanted to visit him but wasn't sure how. The feeling continued, so I drew Lillian and Nan into the journey with me.

I had no idea until that afternoon that both Lillian and Nan were also from the South, with Lillian having grown up in Louisiana and Nan in Kentucky. I grew up in Tennessee, though I had spent the last twenty-nine years in New Jersey.

We discussed the segregated schools of our youth, the "coloreds only" water fountains, access to movie theaters only through the balcony for "colored people." Lillian recalled battling fear when a black man sat next to her on the bus—every message of her culture said she should move. I remembered being told in all sincerity, "Never look a black man in the eye." Such was the racist world in which we cut our teeth, the very air we breathed.

In the same world some of us were cared for by African American women in our homes. These women gave of themselves each and every day, and we grew to love them with a fierce loyalty over the years, even as we recognized the injustice that forced them to nurture us at the expense of their own children's care.

"I guess our Southern roots have a lot to do with why we're going," I observed, not realizing then how true that statement was for me. "I'd like to do something significant for the orphans and Africa, but we need to build relationships and gather facts first. We need to understand what might help the children and what won't. It's not as straightforward as we've been led to believe. Large-scale foreign aid from one government to another is not helping. What *will* make a difference? What could be our call to action? I don't know. I need to go and see for myself."

"I agree, and no matter what we encounter, together the three of us can do this," Lillian said. United in spirit, we hugged one another with unspoken assurances that all would be well as we traveled to a crowded mountain city in Cameroon, with bug spray very much in tow.

CHAPTER 2

Inside Out People

Twenty hours after taking off from Newark Liberty International Airport, we arrived in Cameroon, which is located southeast of Nigeria and is slightly larger than the state of California. When our plane landed at dusk in the city of Douala, we were exhausted but exhilarated and took in the scene. Imagine Newark or O'Hare at rush hour times ten. Imagine being the only faces of your race anywhere in sight. Imagine confusion when the bag carousel doesn't work.

Enter Sister Jane in her flowing white nun's habit with black headpiece, accompanied by Peter and Paul dressed alike in navy shirts and dark slacks. They offered us big hugs and welcome and—with some well-placed bribes—quickly got us and our luggage through customs and onto the paved streets.

The stifling hot air hit me the minute I stepped outside. More chaos. A teeming mass of people in every direction with nowhere to go. Taxis at least thirty years old filled with dents and rust. Fortunately, with Sister Jane in charge we soon spotted the dark blue Good Shepherd van and driver and we were off, chatting like old friends who hadn't seen each other in years.

After maneuvering through streets that were chock-a-block with people in worn, Western clothes, walking or driving rundown cars or motorcycles, we were ushered into the Minotel Vallee des Princes Hotel in the heart of downtown Douala. The hotel was elegant, complete with crystal chandelier, antique furniture, elaborate wall hangings, plush carpet and air-conditioned rooms. Since Douala is located in a French-speaking province, the furniture and food bore the mark of French style in this seemingly out-of-place, upscale hotel. We saw no display of wealth like it throughout the rest of our visit. Not surprisingly, Sister Jane had cut a deal with the hotel.

After a night of sound sleeping, we awoke bright and early, then gathered for breakfast in the hotel's dining area. I was surprised to see Nan and Lillian in their "suburban clothes": Nan wore a turquoise and green blouse and Lillian a nice coral-colored pantsuit. I had done copious research and purchased several pairs of cargo pants in khaki and dark green along with several dark T-shirts with long sleeves. They were obviously not as uptight as I was.

With a hot breakfast in our stomachs and the three of us in our eclectic attire, we were ready to meet the children. But first, we would have to get there. The Good Shepherd Home is located on a hill overlooking Bamenda, Cameroon, a crowded city of almost half a million people. Traveling from Douala on the central coast to Bamenda in the mountainous northwest region is an arduous eight-hour drive on poorly paved, pot-holed roads with no lanes, no speed limit, and no traffic lights. And the motorists? Think New York City taxi drivers on steroids.

We headed from extremely crowded market areas with people in makeshift stalls along the road selling a bit of everything—chickens, vegetables, meat, furniture, flip-flops, and soccer balls—to lush green tropical countryside with beautiful palm and banana plantations that looked like a captivating Caribbean postcard. The contrast was startling and continued unabated throughout our long, tedious journey as we drove from city to market area to countryside then back again.

The heavily crowded market areas we came upon were lined with one stall after another, the more prosperous ones covered with rusty corrugated aluminum roofs, while most were covered in straw. The walls were made of mud bricks, dried in the sun in the shape of concrete blocks and loosely mortared together. Somehow they appeared to have withstood the rainy season.

With more than 50 percent of the population living below the poverty line and an average living wage in Cameroon of less than a dollar a day, very few people have money with which to buy goods, so it's mostly a barter economy, as is the case in many African countries. Everyone seemed to have something to sell or trade; those without stalls plied goods carried on their heads—from food to firewood to hardware supplies.

As our drive continued, I was struck by the crowded conditions. I never saw a motorcycle with less than three people riding on it, and often there were four. Cars and buses were filled beyond capacity, while people without transportation could hardly take a step in the dense crowd without jostling one another. Clearly, there were way too many people crammed in too small a city with little means to support themselves.

Nan turned to Randy, the driver who doubled as the Home's electrician, and asked him, "Why are all those people just sitting on motorcycles over there?"

"They have nowhere to go; they have no jobs, so they're just lined up hoping someone will come offer them something. The government says we have around 30 percent unemployment, but it's actually higher than that. That just counts the people who are still officially looking for work."

We bounced through more uneven potholes, gradually making our way back into a broad expanse of countryside. On such stretches, Randy's breakneck speed along with the open windows sent a refreshing breeze blowing through the van, cooling us on the scorching, sunny day. With the air on our faces and the beat of African music filling our ears, I felt totally free and adventurous.

Suddenly our van veered to the left and made an abrupt stop by the side of the road. A young man, whom Sister Jane seemed to know, came to the door and they began talking animatedly in another language, which I later learned was the Bafut dialect.[1] During the roadside discussion, there was much gesticulating and shaking of heads to indicate "no." After fifteen minutes a boy of about twelve hopped into the van, sat next to us in the back on a small jump seat that had been folded against the door, and off we went.

"The young man I was talking to came down to rent a palm farm for us so we can get palm oil," Sister Jane told us. "We rented it for eight hundred dollars. We use much red palm oil for cooking at the Home; it's so expensive to buy, I had to do something. We are renting this place so we can hopefully get eight hundred liters of palm oil for the year; we use twenty liters every week. This is the brother who will be taking care of the farm. The money we gave him is to clear the farm and to also put in groundnuts [peanuts] for the dry season."

"What were you negotiating with him about?" I asked.

"He was saying the money I gave was not enough to clear the farm and buy the peanut seeds to plant. I said I think the money was enough. He said it wasn't. I told him that since he's gotten married, his wife can help him. He was telling me he cannot do without a wife because the work is too much for him by himself. Some people just get married to get help working the farms. It was about two weeks ago that he got her, a girl of eighteen years. That man is now working the farm and she has to work with him." With that, we bounced down the road with our new passenger.

I tried to make conversation with the boy seated next to us. "My name's Elizabeth. What's yours?" Sitting there in his T-shirt, long beige shorts, and dusty sneakers, he didn't seem to hear me. I repeated my question and he ducked his head, looking afraid.

Sister Jane laughed, "My dear, he has not seen a person like you. He will probably not talk to you."

"Like me how . . . white?"

"White," she responded. "You know, a lot of children like him have never seen a white person. In fact, I have heard white people referred to as 'erased', or 'inside out' or 'peeled' people."

"Inside out! Now that's interesting," I observed. "So tourists must not come here very often. I hadn't realized that."

"Elizabeth, I believe you will learn some things while you are here," Sister Jane noted, smiling.

As the van rolled on, I felt as if a book were unfolding before me. I'm a voracious reader and usually read on a trip of that length. Not this time. What I was seeing and experiencing was far more enlightening than any book I had read, and I was right in the middle of this one.

I was beginning to understand why Cameroon is called "Africa in miniature." We had already driven through a coastal town with beaches and lush tropical plantations; now we were headed for the mountains. The views out our windows were as dramatic as they were interesting. Little did I know just how interesting things would become, even before we pulled into the entrance to the Good Shepherd Home.

Note

1. There are over two hundred fifty different tribes in Cameroon, each with its own dialect.

CHAPTER 3

Gendarmes and Cornfield Excursions

Along the steep, winding road to the orphanage there were at least a dozen security checkpoints. I had read about them in a guidebook which suggested paying the bribes and moving on. Fortunately I was not driving and we were in the hands of experienced locals. At the first few checkpoints, the gendarmes, wearing red berets and green uniforms, waved us on after seeing "The Good Shepherd Home" logo painted in bright yellow on the side of the van. Nonetheless, there were a number of other not-so-friendly-looking checkpoints at which we were motioned to pull to the side of the road.

Initially, a man who was not wearing a uniform motioned for us to stop. In a white shirt, his stomach hanging over his slacks, sweat dripping from his face, he looked into the van and began talking and motioning to Randy and Sister Jane. There was no doubt in my mind that I needed to remain quiet. What concerned me was that the man didn't seem to be with an armed service and could have been anyone who was stopping cars, taking money and who knew what else if he didn't get what he wanted. Fearless, Sister Jane responded in kind; to my surprise, after several minutes they both started laughing. Randy gave him some money and we continued on our way.

"He was just very, very hot and was thinking he needed money to buy some water, the poor man," Sister Jane said, as if the interaction made all the sense in the world. There were several more checkpoints at which Randy got out of the van, paid the gendarmes, and waited for the signal to go through.

Their system for deterring cars that didn't pay the bribes was inventive. Unlike the United States, where there are elaborate spiked mechanisms embedded in the road with warning signs not to back up, they had a simple board with nails sticking up out of it. It lay across the road and was attached to a rope held by a guard. When given the signal the guard jerked the rope, pulled the board to one side and cleared the way. Each time I saw the homemade contraption pulled away, I breathed a bit easier, even knowing there were more just ahead.

"Canon Elizabeth, let me tell you about Nafi," Sister Jane offered, using my official title as a priest who worked for a bishop. After passing through our fifth checkpoint, she seemed to sense that I was eager for news of the child I had come to visit. "Let me tell you about your son."

"My son," I thought. I had two children of my own at home, so I wasn't quite ready for that designation. But I said nothing.

"Nafi came to the Home four years ago when he was five," Sister Jane said. "Then his sister Alexia came a year later and she was thirteen years. She finished primary school but was not willing to work at secondary school. She wanted to learn a trade instead, so we put her to sewing. Then when the other children went back to school, she changed her mind and thought she'd go to school also. So we sent her to school and paid her fees. Then she just abandoned the school and escaped the Home in the middle of the night! She told Nafi to come with her. Nafi said, 'No I am not coming with you.' And it was Nafi who told us the story in the morning. People were asking for Alexia and he said, 'I know, Mama. I will tell you what happened.' So Nafi is still with us. He refused to go with Alexia.

"Nafi's a courageous boy. He loves the Home and he's smart. For a small child like that to say 'no' to his big sister was a really good thing. It was difficult for Alexia out there so she tried to come back to us, but we were afraid she would find ways to take Nafi out, so we said, 'no.'"

"What happened to their parents. Do you know?"

"Yes, I know," Sister Jane sighed. "The parents are dead. Nafi was one year when the mother died. Then the father died when he was two years. I'm not sure what they died of. It may have been AIDS; they don't say, but Nafi has no diagnosis. He is fine."

I was thankful he had somehow found his way to the Home at the age of two, and wondered if he would be alive today if he hadn't.

"My mother saw this poor boy of the Bafut tribe suffering in the village," Sister Jane continued. "He was going from home to home begging for food, so my mother decided to bring him to us. He was the third child who came."

I could not imagine a two-year-old going from one home to another begging for food. Did some people tell him "no"? Did he remember it? I realized I had no idea what his life was like. None at all.

"His father was so nice," Sister Jane said. "I heard when the mother died that the father would get food for Nafi and would not eat himself. So when the father died also it was really sad."

Nafi was still connected to his extended family. He used to visit with his grandmother on holidays, but when she died Sister Jane said he would return to see his aunt. "We try to keep our children in touch with their relatives, so during the big holidays [pronounced 'holy days'], we send the children home for a month. It is very important that they stay connected to the family they have left."

Having read that some Western aid organizations do not favor orphanages since they separate children from their extended families, I was glad to hear that Sister Jane had addressed this concern. She seemed to have a sixth sense for how to provide exactly what the children needed in order to flourish, even if it meant defying routine procedure.

"Sister Jane, if the children have families, why are they in your orphanage?" I asked.

"You see, most of them are members of extended families who are either too poor to care for them or treat them like slaves and refuse to send them to school. A part of what I do is rescue orphaned children from such maltreatment."

"Like slaves?" I repeated.

"Yes, but, not all of the children were mistreated. Take Nafi for instance. His extended family was very loving, but he had no food to eat. They could not care for him in any way, so he came to me. There's also a small percentage of our children who have a parent who's alive, but can't care for them because of a mental or physical illness. So actually our children are either orphaned or abandoned.

"Anyway, Nafi went home for that month and he was with the grandmother. Life there was so hard for him because there was no food. So Nafi was making brooms. He cleaned leaves off palm branches and made brooms with them after they dried. He would go in the bush to get the branches. He saved every penny he earned.

He wouldn't use it to buy food to eat. Then when he came back here after holiday, he told me, 'Mama, this is what I earned from making brooms. This is something to buy my books with, Mama.' His books for school. And with all that work, the amount he earned and gave me is equal to your twenty-five cents. Nafi's the only child among all the children who did that. The only child."

We soon pulled to the right side of the road where I took in the aroma of meat on a nearby grill. "This is where we'll eat lunch."

"The local McDonald's!" joked Lillian.

"It is. This is where everyone eats along the road. In fact, it's the only place like this between Douala and Bamenda." As soon as we pulled to a stop, several people crowded around the van. One woman, with a look of desperation in her eyes, was selling cassava from an orange plastic plate, wrapped in what looked like leaves and string. Others were selling various fruits, and yet another, toothbrushes. We bought lots of cassava for the children; then it was time for lunch.

On the grills were brown paper bags tied with twine, with large pieces of meat cooking inside. "The bag keeps it real juicy," said Sister Jane. "This meat is good, let me tell you."

It was tempting and our mouths were watering, but we passed up the meat and ate bananas and hardboiled eggs instead. If you could peel it, we ate it.

Back in the van, after several minutes of silence, Sister Jane unexpectedly remarked, "Randy, I think this car is having a problem right now and it's the very problem we had before. We may have to hire another car. I don't know if this one will take us because the water is leaking down. We took it to the garage and they said it was okay to take to Douala."

"How did this happen?" I asked, suddenly focused not on food, but on the van. There weren't exactly any Hertz Rent-a-Cars nearby, or even any vehicles that looked better than the one we were already in. In fact, most of them looked worse.

"We paid a mechanic for a good motor," Sister Jane responded, shaking her head and letting out a big sigh. "He took the money and went to Japan to buy one for us. He came back, sold the motor to someone else for a higher price and gave us this bad one."

So we pulled off the road. They had a white plastic gallon jug in the back and there was a stream nearby. They poured water into the engine to cool it down, and then we sped off again at breakneck speed. We repeated this routine every time we were anywhere near a stream, praying each time that the van would start again.

Soon we came to more checkpoints. As we slowed to a stop near one, children surrounded our van selling yellow roasted corn on the cob. "Would you all like some?" Sister Jane asked.

"I would," Nan replied, "but I'm afraid to eat it. We've been told to just eat things we can peel."

"Oh, right, that makes sense for you, but I'm getting one. I love corn."

As Sister Jane was eating her roasted corn on the cob, up walked the first guard I had seen wearing a uniform with a black armband that said, "Police." He was tall, thin, and unlike the gendarmes, carried a large black rifle. He also peered into our van; I just looked down and kept quiet.

As usual, Sister Jane was unperturbed. "Please," she pleaded, "just let these people go through. They're tired. They've traveled a long way. Just let them go through."

The policeman pointed out that he was keeping order in his country, that it was a very safe place because of the police and that we should thank him. Clearly we were not from Africa and he wanted to be certain we saw him as protecting us, rather than threatening. He waved us through. Between the frequent security checkpoints and the overheated van spitting steam, I was concerned we might not reach our destination that day as planned. Fortunately, along the way, Sister Jane kept us entertained with lively conversation about her country, the children, and the Good Shepherd Home. In spite of the cultural differences and the rough, bouncy road, I was filled with a sense of calm and peace—until one unexpected stop.

As you might imagine, there were no roadside toilet facilities, so an eight-hour trip was bound to include what Lillian called a "cornfield excursion." Thanks to her warning, we were armed with supplies.

Lillian and I climbed out of the van and walked down a small hill through dense green undergrowth, checking out potential locations. Fearful of snakes, mosquitoes, and who knew what else, we stepped gingerly and looked about carefully. Lillian found a spot hidden from the road yet not too far away. We were nearly there when a dozen men with machetes appeared, walking down the road just in front of the van. I looked at them; I looked at Lillian; I looked at the position of the van and knew we couldn't make it back before the men were upon us. I had no choice but to stay where I was. Visions of being hacked to death with a machete suddenly flashed before my eyes. Fortunately the thoughts disappeared as fast as they came. I quickly surmised that to act afraid or as if anything were amiss might in fact cause something to become amiss. Panic was not an option.

"Lillian, what do we do?" I asked in a low voice.

"Just stay right here and act like nothing's wrong. Come on; move your feet, Elizabeth. Keep going," she said in a coarse whisper.

I almost froze in my tracks. I was filled with a paralyzing fear, but kept moving as she advised as if nothing were wrong. It was highly likely that the men were simply walking home from working in a field and that they weren't looking for trouble, much less for two American women making a pit stop.

Suddenly they walked up to the driver's side of the van and again I heard unexpected laughter and the exchange of pleasantries. Could Sister Jane know them? I kept walking towards the spot we had selected as if nothing were out of the ordinary and gradually the men passed by above us, disappearing down the road. I was filled with a feeling of calm and peace, when normally I would have been anything but calm. We completed our mission and ran back up the hill as quickly as possible, back through the undergrowth, completely unworried about snakes or other creatures this time.

"What happened, Sister Jane? Did you know those men?" Lillian and I asked breathlessly as we climbed back into the van.

"No, no, my dear, I'd never seen them before. Since I knew you all couldn't get back, I called them to the window and told them they looked like good boys and they looked hungry. They said they were and I gave them some of our food. They thanked us and on they went."

I found myself thinking about Sister Jane and her actions. How could she have thought so quickly without missing a beat, reaching out her hand in love to people who might have done us harm? Later I was to learn how. Sister Jane had faced and overcome much worse than our cornfield pit stop experience.

CHAPTER 4

Joy Unspeakable

"**Come on, baby. Come on, baby.** Come on." I was pleading with the engine of our van, as dusk began to settle into the hills around us. We had made our fifth stop traveling up a steep hill that I had been told was nine miles long.

Once again the engine was hissing and spewing steam, but this time it was into a van that already felt like an oven inside. With sweat beading on my forehead and soaking my clothes, I silently cursed the mechanic who had knowingly cheated the Sisters and the children. And for what? To make a buck? Why them? Because he knew they couldn't tell a good engine from a bad one. Because no Better Business Bureau or police would ever come after him.

"We wish you a Merry Christmas; we wish you a Merry Christmas," chimed Sister Jane's cell phone. I never did figure out why that was the ring in the month of July. "Yes, yes, we're close. Yes. About thirty more minutes now. We're almost there."

Suddenly the engine revved up, and we jumped in the van and rode off at a snail's pace. "That's it!" Sister Jane declared. "We've done it! There's just one more hill and we're there."

This was the dreaded hill Lillian had warned us about, the last hill before arriving at the Home. Fortunately luck was with us; the deeply rutted dirt hill was completely dry, so it was easy to navigate. Never mind the precipitous drop-off with no guard rail to the left, and the dirt and rocks that had tumbled off the hill to the right. The van kept going, veering from right to left and back again.

Then we came around a bend in the road and saw fifty children outside the entrance to the Home, all cheering and jumping up and down. My heart was jumping up and down with them. We drove into the compound past several buildings on the right, a dirt basketball court and cornfield enclosed by a fence covered in laundry on the left, then up a slight incline into a courtyard, as the children, laughing, raced behind the van.

As we climbed out, they swarmed, engulfing us. There were young girls in crinoline party dresses and Mary Janes; older girls in matching white T-shirts and short blue skirts; young boys in shorts and others wearing three-piece suits; older girls in knit hats and younger boys wearing sweaters; teenage boys in sunglasses with shirt tails hanging out; young women with infants in their arms, wearing long pieces of brightly colored African fabric called wrappers. There were children laughing, toddlers crying, children singing, clapping, and stomping their feet in time to music the older children were playing.

One after another, they put their arms around my waist and their heads on my stomach, smiling and welcoming me. There were children wanting to be picked up, and finally, there was Nafi. I recognized this thin nine-year-old boy, only about four feet tall, from his pictures. He looked at me expectantly from the sea of faces as if waiting to be found, ducking his head shyly yet smiling at me with dark brown eyes that seemed too large for his shaved head. He was wearing the outfit I had sent him two years before—shorts, matching shirt, and v-neck vest. We hugged and I kept asking, "How are you? How are you?"

Lillian and Nan held infants in their arms, and all three of us were shedding tears of joy. We had made it, and it felt as if buckets of love were raining down upon us, seeping into our very pores.

Soon each child assembled in the courtyard and we were treated to singing and dancing. The older boys were playing African drums, Sister Jane and the rest of the Sisters were singing, dancing, and clapping, and we savored the unforgettable moment.

After several songs, Nafi came to the front of the group and read a special greeting he had obviously been rehearsing for a long time. He cleared his throat, looked up, and announced, "A speech presented by Nafi Ndika on the occasion of the visit of our mothers, Mama Lizzie, Mama Lillian, and Mama Nancy." Then he continued:

"Our beloved mothers, you are warmly welcome to our home. We are thankful you are safely with us and hope that you will have a happy stay with us," he began, looking self-conscious yet determined to get each and every word just right. Standing stiffly with his head ducked just a bit, he continued.

"Mothers, your presence here brings joy among us. We were very happy when we heard of your coming. Mummy, there is no word that we can thank you for the numerous things you have done for us. Not only thinking about me but the entire Home. We were really in great pains when we were schooling out of the Home. Thanks to God that you have provided us with a comfortable place that we have a good, sound, and comfortable education. We were regarded outside as the rejected ones but you prove to us that we have mothers. It is not easy to live all the way in America and to come and visit us.

"Many thanks to you for the Rabbitory you provided, where we keep all our rabbits, and for the truck your friend gave which helps transport our things and us.

"May you have a safe journey back to America when our time here together is complete.

"Long live our mothers. Long live our Good Shepherd Home. And long live Africa."

Everyone clapped and cheered as Nafi beamed proudly. I could see the relief in his big, dark eyes. He had done it. His English had been perfect, as he profusely thanked us for the little we had done.

"You know, it's the highest regard for children to call a grown woman 'mother' or 'auntie' here in Africa. They have given you a great respect," Sister Jane whispered to us.

We nodded our heads, overwhelmed by our welcome.

"Come, Canon, come; you must see the school building you built for us," Sister Jane then said with a gleam in her eye.

"You know, Sister Jane, the children just called me 'Mama Lizzie.' It's the first time I've ever been called that and I like the sound of it. Why don't you call me 'Mama Lizzie' instead of 'Canon'? 'Canon' seems so formal."

"But it's a big deal to me that you're a canon in the church, next to a bishop. I want to show the honor I feel for you."

"Oh, Sister Jane, I know you honor me and I hope you know that I honor you, too. So how about 'Mama Lizzie'?"

"Okay, Canon, I mean, Mama Lizzie. I will do it, but come see the school you built for us."

I was embarrassed over the lavishness of her praise for my small offering. Many different groups and individuals had contributed to the success of the Home; I was just one of them. But it wasn't every day I had the opportunity to help start a school, and I was excited to see it.

About a year before, I had received an e-mail from Sister Jane detailing the need for a room to house sewing machines so the older children could learn a trade and earn much-needed money. I quickly e-mailed back, "How much is needed?"

"Six thousand dollars" was her unexpected reply.

Six thousand dollars will hardly buy a used car in the United States, much less a building; so after some soul-searching I wired the money to her. Approximately six months later, I received another e-mail. The primary school children were being mistreated at their school in the local village because they were AIDS orphans, the rejected ones. Several of the teachers were abusing them both physically and verbally, assuming they had no one to stand up for them.

Little did they know the firestorm they had unleashed. With her dignified sense of presence and determined conviction, Sister Jane marched into the principal's office demanding fair treatment for her children. After a great deal of denial from the school and nothing materially changing, she turned the sewing room into a primary school. For a long time I had envisioned the small, one-room school and was thankful that it had been ready for them when they needed it.

To my delight, it was much more than just one room. Imagine five rooms plus an apartment with indoor plumbing all for six thousand dollars. Sister Jane hadn't told me how far the money had stretched, and she delighted in surprising me.

In the main room there were small, obviously hand-made wooden desks, neatly arranged in rows with tattered, old books spilling out. I wondered who had sent the books and what children in what country had used them before. The blackboards at the front of the room were not black but blue with the last history lesson still posted: "What is the slave trade? What is slavery? Who fought for the abolition of the slave trade? What is the triangular slave trade?"

They were learning the history of their people, a tragic history of abuse and domination of one human being over another leading to the breakup of families on one end, certain death for many in transit, and a life of dehumanization, back-breaking labor, physical abuse, and servitude on the other, the effects of which are still in existence throughout the world. They were learning the truth of our shared past.

"The building in front of us is where the children sleep, and up these stairs on the left are your guest quarters," Sister Jane told us with a broad smile. "Come."

We climbed the stairs and entered a series of lovely rooms. Not only did we each have our own bedroom with colorful flowered blankets and fluffy pillows; but there was a sitting area with meticulously sewn blue drapes edged in white lace; a wooden couch and chairs with bright tropical fabric seats in yellows, pinks, and blues; and joy of joys, indoor plumbing. Sister Jane had even had a hot water heater installed in the bathroom of the convent so we could walk there to take a hot bath.

And there was more. When we arrived at the convent for dinner, we discovered that she had hired a chef from a local hotel to cook for us. How delighted we were to have fish soup, African chicken peanut stew,[1] green beans and carrots, and hash brown potatoes for our dinner, a dinner filled with eye-opening conversation with our host, Sister Jane. As the meal ended, we said our goodnights.

Sister Jane's dream of saving orphans' lives had become reality, a reality we were privileged to live into at that moment. With full bellies and joy unspeakable in our hearts, we walked with our flashlights, called torches, back down the packed dirt road to our quarters for a night of very sound sleep.

Note

1. For recipes for Cameroonian Fish Soup, African Chicken Peanut Stew, and more African treats, go to *www.elizabethgeitz.com* and click on "I Am That Child."

CHAPTER 5

Mealtime Tutorial

I awakened on my first morning in the Home to what sounded like an Indian chant, along with bells ringing, roosters crowing, and children laughing. This certainly beat my alarm clock at home in America.

When we came into the courtyard, Sister Jane was standing outside with two of the children, exuding quiet confidence and strength in the midst of the many demands on her time.

"Sister Jane, good morning," I called. "I can hardly believe we're finally here. Did you hear that chanting? I woke up feeling like I was in India instead of Africa. What was that?"

"That was the imam calling the Muslims to prayer. They're all over Cameroon, particularly here in the North Region. About twenty percent of Cameroon's population is Muslim and about forty percent is Christian."

"So how does that work since this is a Christian orphanage?" I asked. "I'm guessing you have children from different faith traditions here."

"We respect children of all faiths or no faith. We would never baptize a child without their extended family's permission," she replied, matter-of-factly. That was encouraging. Some faith-based orphanages in developing nations have a clear mission of proselytizing vulnerable children.

With that settled, we walked to the convent together, entering a large sitting room filled with overstuffed furniture trimmed in African wood with hand-crocheted doilies on the head rests and arms. Pictures of previous guests graced the wall above the couch. A large dining table and chairs were on the left; on the opposite side a table with a laptop computer rested against the wall next to a group of locally made bamboo and cane chairs in a large circle. As we took in our surroundings, our eyes landed on a glorious sight: three babies, bathed and wrapped in clean clothes and blankets. Two were contentedly sleeping in the corner of the couch, almost purring, while the last infant was being fed by one of the Sisters.

Sister Jane explained to us their ingenious way of figuring out what to feed the babies. "We went up to several mothers who had healthy-looking babies and asked them what they fed them. One mother said, 'Oh Sister, let me tell you what I do. I take corn, roast it; take soybeans, roast it; take powdered crayfish, roast everything together, and grind it all up with groundnuts into a powder.' Then in the morning we mix it with sugar and hot water and put it in the feeding bottle," she finished. "It's called pap [pronounced 'pop']."

We decided they had American baby food beat hands down. Not once did we see a baby spit up or hear a colicky baby. Not once did we see a baby who didn't gulp it down and look as content as the cat who ate the cream.

After breakfast I went into the sitting room and picked up one of the babies dressed in pink and wrapped in a blanket, resting against the arm of the couch where she had been laid. I couldn't believe how lightweight she was. She felt like a balloon, yet appeared to be healthy.

"What's her name?" I asked, peering into her perfect tiny face, almost doll-like, and noting her dainty fingers and plaited hair.

"Joelle," replied Sister Jane, "and oh, that baby. You would not believe her when she came here. Her feet! They were rotten with open sores and that child had pneumonia. It was horrible. When the baby arrived, Sister Mary Lynne was here from the Episcopal convent in New Jersey. She said, 'Get this child to the hospital immediately.' She thought Joelle would die. I told her, 'Sister, we are used to this kind of thing.' So in the morning, we took her to the hospital. They discovered she had pneumonia; they started a treatment and you see how she is now.

"The doctor gave us something to use on her feet. That baby had a fungus. Joelle would have died if she had not been brought here. No question—she would have died," Sister Jane noted with an ominous tone. I was beginning to sense both the fragility and sacredness of life in a developing nation. Simply to be alive and well was an accomplishment.

"The mother of that child is alive," she continued. "She is an epileptic patient and many times she is not fine. It goes up in the mind. So she just abandoned the child and was moving, moving, on the street. For one whole night that child never had anything except water. The father did not know what to do with her. For two months he just cried, 'Who will help with this child?' People told him, 'Take the child up to the orphanage. Take the child to the Good Shepherd Home.' So that tiny child came here."

"How much do you think she weighed then?" Nan inquired.

"I don't know. That child was so tiny, almost dead. She's six months now and she only weighs six and a half pounds. But we're not certain of any of their ages, really. We just have to guess."

As I held Joelle tighter, this perfectly formed baby girl who had survived against all odds, the tragedy of her short life descended upon me like a cloud. There were no safety nets, no government programs for orphans just like her. If Sister Jane had not been here, Joelle would be dead from neglect, starvation, and illness.

Now that I knew, what was I called to do? I had no idea. So I held Joelle, overwhelmed with gratitude for her life and for Sister Jane as we left our first mealtime tutorial.

CHAPTER 6

Learning Your Place

"Come, Canon," Sister Jane coaxed as we were leaving breakfast, then quickly added, "I mean, Mama Lizzie. Right now I want to show you the dormitory we're building for the children on the land Lillian's friend gave us."

We took off down the road as she called to Lillian and Nan to join us. On the right when we drove into the Home and just past the guest quarters, there were two large cement block structures under construction with sand, wood, and wheelbarrows nearby.

Sister Jane immediately introduced us to Divine, a thirty-eight-year-old school teacher who serves as the dormitory construction manager. We then met her cousin Laurence, a civil engineer who works on the project and whatever else is needed at the Home. Wearing a navy T-shirt and floppy brown hat, Laurence appeared to be in his late twenties. As they joined us, we climbed up the soon-to-be-steps together and into the structure.

"Now this large room on the left will be the activities room for making crafts and doing projects. They have no place like this now," Sister Jane said with pride.

"It seems to me they need a quiet room. There's no place for them to study," observed Lillian.

"You know, they can go up there any time they want." Sister Jane pointed in the direction of the Primary School. "Other children from the area come up there because they know it's so quiet; so our children know they can do it."

"I just worry about them trying to study in their rooms," Lillian insisted. "It's so tight in there, with sometimes as many as four of them sleeping in one bunk bed, especially the older boys. I don't see how they do it."

"They know the blackboards are up there. I don't know why they're not using them."

"They need to be encouraged," Lillian replied.

"You know Lillian; you keep talking, talking. Sometimes I am exhausted," sighed Sister Jane, shaking her head with weariness.

We all howled with laughter, for suddenly we knew exactly what we were doing. Right. We knew more about what the children needed than she did. She was correct to bring us up short and thankfully it was the first and only time she did. At that moment, we learned who was in charge, if in fact there'd ever been any doubt.

"Ok, I'll be quiet," said Lillian. "From what you're saying, it sounds like they work it out somehow among themselves."

"You know, since I've been here I can really see them in a room like this when school's not in session making crafts and jewelry as you say, like at a camp in the United States," I suggested.

"Very soon they begin harvesting crops," Sister Jane explained. "Then they will be very busy so they can have food to eat." In other words: no summer camp here. This was about survival.

"Now is this the entrance hall?" I asked, moving into the space outside the activity room. As soon as the words were out of my mouth, I realized the privilege imbedded in them. Who had the luxury to build entrance halls?

"This is going to be an apartment for our dorm mother," Sister Jane answered patiently. "We hope to have a kitchen, toilet, sitting area, and bedroom." As we had come to realize, an arrangement like this would be luxurious in Cameroon.

Next we walked to the rear of the first floor. Pointing to a large room, Divine explained that it would be the refectory, or dining hall. A man was just beginning to paint large, colorful murals on the walls to brighten the space.

"You know what occurs to me," I offered, still trying to be helpful, "when it gets to a certain stage, volunteers from the United States could come here and work, like with Habitat for Humanity. Am I right, Lillian?"

"It's a bit far, Elizabeth; it's not realistic" she answered, with the wisdom of someone who was on her seventh trip to Africa.

"That's right," Sister Jane added. "In fact with so many people out of work, part of our mission is to employ local workers, contribute to the economy that way. On a project of this scope, volunteers wouldn't be much help."

"Got it," I replied and I did. It had taken us two full days to travel here, not to mention the armed checkpoints. I couldn't see many people embracing that, plus the price tag of the round-trip ticket.

"Has all the electrical work been done?" asked Nan.

"No, not yet, but it's all accounted for. We have the funds, but you know what happened? We had the cables all in and they came and pulled them out."

"Who?"

"Thieves!" Sister Jane, Laurence, and Divine all retorted in unison. "They rip them out to resell them."

As if thievery were an everyday occurrence, Divine then calmly pointed out a pantry, an indoor kitchen with serving area, and an outdoor kitchen surrounded by a beautiful stone wall. Sister Jane explained that the wall was to separate the outdoor kitchen from the chicken farm they planned to construct.

We then walked down makeshift stairs to the second level, all above ground because the building was situated on a very steep hill. It was dark and damp inside the concrete walls, but there was still enough light to see. We walked into the girl's dormitory area where there were lots of individual rooms. Every room would have two bunk beds with space for four girls, giving each her own mattress—certainly better than the current three to four children per mattress. There would also be a wardrobe for each child in the hall, secured to the wall. Presently they had no closets or dressers, just trunks or old suitcases with their few belongings inside.

There was even space for showers at each end of the floor along with indoor toilets. I wasn't aware of it at the time, but I later learned that none of the children had ever had the sheer pleasure of taking a hot shower or bath. Bath time for children of all ages was in buckets of cold water in a small, cement courtyard outside their living quarters. They loved to splash one another, playing and giggling during bath time, with toddlers slipping out of the grasp of the older children who were bathing them. They didn't know the difference; there was nothing to compare it to. Soon they would enjoy two showers at each end of the girls' floor heated by solar energy, and two showers at each end of the boys' floor.

"Our plan is that after the children leave here they will go to a boarding school we are hoping to build in town," Sister Jane explained. "One of our donors has already raised money for the first phase of construction. It will be the equivalent of a United States high school where the children can go for more advanced studies, so they can pass their entrance exams for university."

As our tour continued it was becoming clear that Sister Jane was not only a visionary with boundless energy, but a shrewd business woman who could effortlessly multi-task in various arenas and share her gifts with those around her.

We continued down another set of stairs into the boys' sleeping quarters, an exact duplicate of the girls' area upstairs. The plan was for each floor to accommodate forty children. Again, we were above ground on the steep incline, but it was darker than the floor just above it. Fortunately there was a bare light bulb hanging from the ceiling by a wire, and Divine turned it on.

"Some men are here to see you from the electric department, Sister Jane," called out one of the older boys, and suddenly there was a man peering through one of the door openings above us.

"Sir, we had a problem and they are fixing it up. When they fix it up, we will pay the amount we are supposed to pay," Sister Jane called to him.

"We will have to cut your lights off!" he answered loudly.

"No, that is not possible. I am saying that I have complained about this; that there is a problem. How can you be insisting this?" she continued, her volume rising to match his.

I couldn't hear all of the man's reply but the words "disconnect" and "tomorrow morning" came through loud and clear. Divine and Laurence joined in the discussion, and again, to my complete surprise, Sister Jane chuckled a bit.

After they left she explained, "We have not paid. The bills were too high. We went to complain, and they took our paper to check why our bills had doubled. They say they will look at it today and try to fix the problem, otherwise they say they will come tomorrow morning and disconnect."

"I've got to go work on the pigs now," said Laurence, unfazed by the possibility of a power shut off. "I need to make room for the ones I will be picking up tomorrow. I have to leave at four o'clock in the morning to get them because pigs are allergic to the sun and will die if they get too hot."

That was news to me.

"That's why you always hear of pigs rolling in the mud, to keep cool," offered Lillian. "So at four in the morning they're off to get ten pigs."

"I will sell some of them," Laurence told us, as we continued our tour around the grounds. "We sold some before. We used to have about seventy pigs. I'll show you their pen tomorrow; it's down a steep hill. Now, here we are at the Rabbit Farm."

So this was the Rabbit Farm, or what Nafi called the Rabbitory. Laurence explained that they had to build a tall fence around it because the dogs were getting in and eating the rabbits.

"Mobiya and Cyrille, two of our teenage boys, are in charge of the rabbits and they've named them."

"How do they eat them then?" I asked.

"My father grew up on a farm," interjected Nan, "and they raised pigs. My father had named one of them. Then at breakfast one morning his father told him, 'Enjoy Wilbur.'"

Some things are, indeed, universal.

CHAPTER 7

Poison

After a lunch of leftover soup from the night before, we were ready for a long nap. How much we had learned in one morning alone! As I lay in bed that afternoon listening to the children playing outside my window, I realized I had not been prepared for the degree to which some people in this community preyed upon one another. First was the man who cheated the Sisters out of the reliable engine they had purchased, substituting one with inadequate horsepower. Then there were the thieves who had stolen the cables once they were installed in the new dormitory, as well as those who regularly stole firewood the Home used for cooking. Because Sister Jane was so tough and savvy, she knew how to fight back, but it was a daily battle.

With these thoughts swirling through my head, I was in awe at the unbridled joy of the children and people of all ages in this country—their spirit, their hope in the face of bleak realities, and yes, their exuberant gratitude and faith.

So many people in America have lost their joy, as well as their sense of spiritual well-being, in the midst of material abundance. I knew there was a connection between the two that merited further exploration, but at that moment, I could hardly keep my eyes open.

Rain began to fall steadily on our tin roof, the perfect condition for taking a nap. Two hours later we awoke refreshed, ready to spend time with the children. I couldn't wait to look for Nafi. As the sun began to set, I found him outside; we just talked and walked around holding hands. He is a polite, shy boy and I wondered if my initial enthusiasm had overwhelmed him.

The previous night, I had given him a soccer ball I had brought in my carry-on luggage. He seemed to like it, even though it immediately disappeared with some of the older boys. I had also brought him one of my favorite children's books called *Old Turtle*. I read part of it to him and we called it a night.

The next afternoon, I quickly sensed that more than the soccer ball or book, Nafi seemed most excited about the picture of my family I had pasted in the book with a hand-written note from each of us. So I talked a bit about Charlotte, our twenty-eight-year-old daughter, and Mike, our twenty-year-old son, who also liked soccer. I told him about my husband of thirty-four years, Michael, who enjoyed spending time in the great outdoors. Nafi didn't say much that afternoon; he just held my hand tightly and seemed glad to have me next to him. I looked forward to laying the groundwork for an ongoing relationship with him, so I could provide the extra support he would need financially, as well as spiritually and emotionally, in the years ahead.

Sister Jane had been clear from the outset that the children of the Good Shepherd Home are to remain in Africa, receive care and schooling with the Sisters, and become its next generation of leaders. Removing the brightest, well-schooled children from a country through adoption does nothing to help the country. Sister Jane's goal was the transformation of Africa, not just putting Band-Aids on deep, systemic issues.

The motto of the Good Shepherd Home is "May We All Be One." A significant part of Sister Jane's vision is to bring together orphans from all the tribes in her country under one roof. With tribal infighting, and some groups looking down on others as less than human, she believes that helping children see all people as brothers and sisters, as one, could do nothing less than transform the future of her country. These children would have the values, education, work ethic, and love for their fellow Africans necessary to change the course of history. I was honored to be a small part of her ambitious undertaking.

As we gathered before dinner that evening, Nan, Lillian, and I shared how moved we were by their hospitality. They had left no stone unturned in their lavish welcome and we were concerned about the amount of effort they were exerting on our behalf. We had insisted on paying for all our expenses and then some, but their care for us went beyond mere dollars and cents.

"Sister Jane, we're here to help you," we insisted. "Let us cook for the children or bathe the babies, something."

"No, my dear, no. We have many helping hands, more than enough. Plus the Sisters and the orphans all have their routines. It would just confuse things. You come, you stay with us, you are our guests. It is really a kind of prestige for us to have Americans stay here. Everybody is just happy around, because we have our guests."

"But we're not guests," we protested. "We're here to help."

"The way you can help most is to learn as much as possible about us. Help us determine which projects we need next and how to get them started. We need your resources. We need your knowledge of how to get things done. We need your prayers. And we need you to go back to America and get more people involved.

"Besides," she reminded us, "you're going to set up the computers you brought and teach the children how to use them, and you've been reading to them. That's a big help, let me tell you. And just spending time with the children, letting them know you love them. That's what they need most."

I was beginning to understand her perspective, but it took some adjustment for all three of us. Sister Jane seemed almost offended when we tried to engage in what she thought of as menial labor, as if we would not let her be our host. We decided it was important not to force our perspective on her and to let her handle our visit in her own way.

"Oh, and the children! Two months before you came all they talked about was your coming," Sister Jane assured us. "It's a big deal to them that you're here and your support means everything to them. They prepared songs and a dance for your last night here. You can give them your gifts then."

We had brought a set of pencils for each child with their full name on each one in gold letters. We could hardly wait to give them out. We wanted to bring them something that was theirs alone to keep and hopefully to remember us by, long after we were gone.

"Sister Jane, I have a friend named Lydia who gave me two hundred dollars to buy something special for the children," Lillian said. "What would you suggest?"

"Oh, tell her the story about that," said Nan, "I love it."

"Well, Lydia is in her late eighties, about 4'11" tall, always wears a bun on the back of her head, and is a feisty, tell-it-like-it-is woman. She was outraged when [former president] George W. [Bush] gave everyone a tax refund. She said the government could not afford to give that money back to people and she refused to spend it on the U.S. economy. So she told me to take it all to Africa and buy something the kids could use."

"Oh, I like that woman! She's my kind!" Sister Jane laughed. "Well . . . the children would love an amplifier."

"An amplifier?" asked Lillian. "That hardly seems like something they really need. I don't know; let me think about it."

"They would love that; I will tell you."

Lillian was hesitant.

"Well, think about it," Sister Jane suggested, clearly hopeful that Lillian would come around. Then she switched gears.

"I need to tell you all something. There are some people who definitely don't like us being here," Sister Jane announced. "Two years ago one of the men from the village even tried to poison me."

Unflappable Lillian calmly explained, "If you get rid of Sister Jane, then the whole thing will fall apart."

"So the target is first me," Sister Jane continued. "They have tried that and failed. An old man from the village brought me some plantain chips one day, and I was scared to eat them because I had heard he did not like me. So I just took them and put them outside; in the morning I went and looked at them. I saw this powdery thing on top, all red, that had been eating the plantains, eating, eating. That poison he put on those chips would have been eating my heart. I showed it to people and they were horrified.

"The next day the man came to visit again and saw that I was fine. I came out and greeted him, and gave him some food to eat. He then handed me something to drink and said, 'Please, please drink it. Drink it while I am here. I want you to taste this in my presence so I can see whether you like it or not.' I would not drink it; I said my stomach was hurting. He said, 'No, just taste it.' I told him, 'I am sorry; I can't. I don't think I want to taste it. I don't feel good.'"

As I listened to Sister Jane's story, my blood ran cold. Yet, she related it as if attempted murder were an everyday occurrence, almost normative.

"They know that money is coming into this place and there are some who are jealous," she continued, seemingly unfazed. "They spread rumors about me, trying to discredit me, spreading my name everywhere. He told this to some shopkeepers in town who started charging us double for everything we tried to buy. I started asking questions and found out that this man had been telling people that we had a lot of money. So I did not trade at those places anymore.

"There are some very good people in Africa, but not everybody," Sister Jane admitted. "There's still a lot of witchcraft here. First was the man who used it to try to get rid of us, then this man who tried to poison me. That's also a type of witchcraft."

"You know, Sister Jane, I was surprised to hear that some of the Sisters believe in witchcraft," I said. "It seems like as Christians they would have a different belief system."

"Not really, Mama Lizzie. Many Christians have still not been able to overcome their fear of witchcraft. It's based on fear of death, fear of failure, fear of illness. Even people educated in the West believe that a village elder can kill your soul while you sleep through the use of witchcraft. So on the one hand the Sisters believe in God, but on the other they fear the power of witchcraft."

That was news to me. I had assumed that one took the place of the other. Apparently not.

"That's partially why a lot of people here don't progress much. I'm not talking about the Sisters; they just fear it, but others still practice it. That's why you see so many Africans running to America to get away from all that. Also, people like that man who tried to poison me don't like that I'm a woman leading this orphanage. That represents a progress they don't like. They say, 'Can you imagine a woman doing all of that?'"

"Oh, because you're a woman you shouldn't be in a position of authority?" I asked.

"Well, now, you've run into that haven't you, Elizabeth?" quipped Lillian.

"Well, yes that's true, but nobody's ever tried to poison me because of it," I said.

"Yes, we give a lot of people jobs and you know, one man we hired poisoned one of our dogs," Sister Jane said, returning to her original topic. "The dog was good in the night and in the morning it was dead. We called the vet and he said, 'Sister, they have poisoned this dog!'"

"How do you bear up under all of this?" I asked. "How do you do it?"

"My dear, don't worry about me," she said. "I am fine. They will never get us . . . I don't think."

As we walked back to our rooms in the cool mountain air with our torches beaming a cone of light in front of us, two security guards walked beside us, one of whom had been hired just for our visit. I was glad to see he had a rifle; I fervently hoped he wouldn't need to use it.

PART II

Listening with the Ear of the Heart

"There is no keener revelation of a society's soul than the way it treats its children."

—*Nelson Mandela*

"Love is such a powerful instrument to make people feel at home."

—*Jane Mankaa*

CHAPTER 8

Weaving Strands
of Pain

How do I sing a song or tell a story in a strange land? With
a clear sense that it is not my story to tell but theirs. With great
awareness of the differences between our cultures and with humility
because I will miss more nuanced emotions and meanings. So I begin
sharing the stories of this amazing community with respect and awe.

It has to begin with Sister Jane. One morning, Lillian, Nan, and
I walked together down the concrete steps leading from our guest
quarters into the courtyard outside the children's rooms, out the iron
gate, and onto the already swept beaten-earth road. We trudged up
the small hill, past the unfinished dormitory on the right, into the
courtyard ahead. Roosters were crowing as children scurried about,
busy with their well-defined daily chores.

"Ah, there you are," exclaimed Sister Jane with an infant in her
arms. "I've been waiting for you."

"And we're ready for you," began Lillian. "We were just wondering . . . what was your childhood like? What was it like for you
growing up in Africa?"

"Oh, you want my life story?" she asked us, grinning. "Okay, let
me give this baby to Mankaa, who works with the little ones. We'll
talk while we eat."

"Well, alright . . . let me begin with the history of my family," she said as we settled into our chairs. "It doesn't start with me.
First of all, my grandfather was the son of a slave woman who was
captured into slavery when the upper Bafut people of Cameroon
went to war with the lower Bafut. After the lower Bafut people
were defeated, they carried the young women north and among
them was my grandfather's mother. When she was twelve years,
she was given to the fon [chieftain or king] of Bafut to stay in

the palace as one of his many wives. The fon selected the ones he wanted and gave the rest of the women to his brothers. My great-grandmother was not selected so she was then given to my great-grandfather in marriage."

"So your great-grandmother had no say in this whatsoever," Lillian said. "She was treated like property."

"Worse than that. She was a captured slave, lower than a piece of property. That's how women and children were treated in war," Sister Jane explained.

"They were the spoils of war," added Nan.

"Like that exactly," Sister Jane confirmed. So she gave birth to my grandfather and four other children. Then my grandparents got married and had eight children. My father is one of them. As for my mother's side, very little is known. She never knew her mother because she died when my mother was about two years. Then her father died when she was eight."

"So your mother was an orphan?" I asked, not expecting this revelation.

"Yes, my mother was an orphan," Sister Jane answered softly, nodding her head. "She started staying with different families then, helping to nurse their children in exchange for food. She had a very difficult life. She used to tell us some of her sad stories, how she was treated and how sometimes she would spend the night under trees.

"She came to marry my father through the intervention of my aunt Mami Mary. When the two women met each other at a bottle dance party, my aunt asked my mother if she would marry her brother."

"What's a bottle dance party?" asked Nan.

"Oh, you've never heard of the Cameroon bottle dance? We're famous for it. There's a man named John Minang who still makes it famous today. He sings songs and makes videos of it. It's even on YouTube. The very type of dance that my mother attended that night is on YouTube. I will show you tonight when the computers are on.

"Okay," Sister Jane continued. "My mother accepted the pro-posal of marriage without ever seeing my father. This is how they got together. No marriage certificate, no court or church wedding, only the traditional marriage conducted with a lot of palm oil poured out on my mother. This is not unusual here in Africa.

"We have a saying that goes, 'Whenever you both go to the bed, don't come back empty. Come back with a child each time you sleep together.' I am that child. I am the first child of eight in my family.

"The sad stories of my mother as an orphan had a lot of impact on me. She would tell us Bible stories and how we should always love God and love one another. Then one day someone else's mother died in our village, leaving behind five children. My mother took two of the oldest and they went to my mother's farm. She would harvest cassava and vegetables and give it to them. We were so poor, but my mother worked very hard to see that we had food to eat, even though we never ever got to eat to our satisfaction.

"My father could have cared less about us. My mother did almost all the farm work and also took care of the children along with other people's children who came to stay in our little house. My mother would never drive anyone away.

"I remember one incident in our home. There was a man who had no place to stay. To make things worse he had epilepsy. For this reason nobody wanted him. One evening he came to our house. He did this because every time he came by, I would call to him and give him something to eat.

"One night he came when my father had already gone to bed; my mother was so happy to welcome him. He sat on a bed near the door. My mother prepared some food for us all and gave him his own. After he ate he told my mother he was feeling very cold, so my mother asked him to come closer to the fire. After about five minutes he had a terrible seizure. He fell on the fire, and my poor mother tried to rescue him by herself.

"I went out to call for my father who came in, but instead of helping my mother rescue that man, he began yelling. He was asking my mother where in this village had she ever seen this man, in someone's home? He then asked what was my mother trying to show. He said my mother would have to spend the night in there with that man. After all the insults at my mother, he took us and left my mother and the man inside the kitchen. He told us he was going to have my mother beaten the next day. He blamed her for bringing in an epileptic man to contaminate his children with epilepsy.

"I felt so sorry for my mother. I cannot imagine how she could stay with my father after all the maltreatment. But my mother would say that she valued her children so much that she would stay with my father. Even if it meant death for her, she would stay.

"We all marvel at my father today because he has changed a lot in his old age. He tells my mother now that all the blessings he has in this life are through her. I am not sure he has ever apologized to her, though. It was my mother's strong faith that gave her the courage she needed to survive."

We sat in silence, our uneaten breakfast in front of us, trying to absorb all we had just heard.

"Now you're saving other orphaned children who sleep under trees or on the streets," Lillian said.

Sister Jane nodded her head.

"And I see why you told us you want to start a special home for children with epilepsy, so you can help children like that man," Nan observed. "It all fits together. You're weaving all these strands of pain into a beautiful fabric."

"Yes, my mother has shown me the way. She has put this in my heart. There was an empty place inside me until I could do something to help others like her and the man she helped, but whatever I can do, it is not enough."

"But Sister Jane, look at what you're doing. Look at all you've accomplished. Just listen to the children outside. Where would they be if it weren't for you?" I said, emphatically.

"Most likely, they would be dead," Lillian said.

Just then three-year-old Franck walked up, wearing a girl's red and white dress and no shoes. "Sister Jane, I just have to ask you this," I said, shifting my attention to a lighter subject. "Is Franck a girl?"

"No, no, Mama Lizzie, Franck's not a girl," she laughed, clearly glad to have some comic relief. "Franck, show Mama Lizzie you're not a girl!" With that, Franck giggled, pulled up his dress and with nothing on underneath, it was plain to see that Franck was indeed a boy. Franck continued to giggle at our obvious amusement.

"Then why has he worn a dress for the last two days?" asked Nan.

"Oh, they don't care. They just put on whatever clothes fit them. They don't have their own clothes so they just share everything," Sister Jane answered, revealing just one more reality of life in an orphanage.

"How old are you Franck?" I asked. Franck held up three fingers. "When's your birthday?"

"Oh, we don't know exactly when their birthdays are," explained Sister Jane, "so on the first of January every year all the children turn a year older. It's easier to keep track of that way. I've got to go now," she added. "You all finish up and I'll tell you the rest of my story another time."

And off she went to begin another day.

CHAPTER 9

Mobiya Dibango

Fourteen-year-old Mobiya has endured what no child should have to endure. His life has been one of tragic loss and hardship. Yet self-pity is not part of his makeup. An excellent student who each day helps the younger children who are now part of his family, he has an infectious smile and his helping hands are a study in motion. Wearing red soccer shorts down to his knees, a faded black T-shirt, and sunglasses, Mobiya could have been a teenager anywhere.

"I'm from a polygamous family," he began, eager to tell me his story. "My mother was the second wife to my father. Since my father died when I was an infant, my mother took all of her children to Douala to live where she thought we would be alright. But life was hard there; it was not easy for her to take care of all of us.

"You see, there are fifteen children in my family; eight by my father's first wife and seven by my mother. We are all of the Wum tribe. When my father died, the first wife took her children to stay with her family and my mother took us to Douala. While we were there, my brother Emmanuel and I used to sleep outside on the ground, on the streets. Our mother could not take care of us all; she was unable to feed us. It was very difficult for her. That's why she took us to stay with her mother. She thought her mother would be able to help us."

There was no trace of sadness in Mobiya's voice, no look of devastation in his eyes. Perhaps Mobiya had felt it for so long that he was numb. He went on.

"Because my mother could not feed us, my uncle came and took three of us to his village to live and work for him—me, Emmanuel, and Mary. My mother thought we would be fine, but things were not going fine. Life there was so horrible! He made us do back-breaking labor all day to support him and his family, while we went without enough food to eat. Many days I was so hungry I thought I was going to pass out, but I still had to keep working, keep going. I used to do business for my uncle as well, and we were not allowed to go to school. Instead, we worked from sunup to sundown.

"My mother had taught us how to bake flour into 'gateaux,' cake; the cakes were plain but sweet, with no icing because it would have melted in the sun. Anyway, that's what we did to earn money. Then my mother fell sick, and Emmanuel and I had to leave my uncle's home to take care of her. I do not know what she was sick with but it was very terrible," he shared, shaking his head.

Each child I spoke with told me they didn't know what their parents had died of, even though according to Sister Jane they were all aware that their parents had died of AIDS. It is a tremendous taboo throughout Africa to have a family member die of AIDS. Acknowledging the cause of death only added to the orphans' being further rejected by their remaining family and friends, even though the orphans at the Good Shepherd Home were not infected themselves. AIDS was the unspoken killer of their parents.

"My mother died in my hands," Mobiya continued more softly, "at night, at two o'clock in the night. I was holding her. My grandmother sent us to the next village to tell my mother's family she had died. We had to go that night to tell them. There was no place to keep the corpse cold, no morgue, so we had to leave right then. We left at four o'clock in the morning to go tell her family in the next village. We were trekking for two hours to get there and at first we were in total darkness. We stumbled and made our way as best we could through thick undergrowth in some places and muddy roads in others. I fell several times and my leg was bleeding from hitting a rock."

He checked to see that I was still listening. I nodded, letting him know that no matter what he had to say, I was a person who could hear it.

"We had to pass through rushing water, through a river," he explained, his voice getting louder. "I was very afraid. The water was full and moving so fast; several times I went under and thought I might not make it. To keep our dresses dry we had to remove them.[1] We had to wrap them up. Our grandmother had told us not to get our clothes wet, so she gave us a wrapper. We were to remove our dresses and tie them in the wrapper, so we did and somehow, even though my head went under, I was able to hold my clothes up high in the air and they stayed dry.

"We finally got to the next village to see our aunt, my father's sister, but nobody was there so we had to wait, wait, wait. She never came. Finally, we sent other people to go look for her in the next village; she was at a farm. Emmanuel and me and my older sister Yvonne made the trip. Then we left to come back to my grandmother's and by that time the river had died down; the water wasn't a problem.

"My mother was buried the next day. My aunt came, but she was late; my mother was already buried, so my aunt and that family never saw her body. Then a fight broke out. My uncle from my father's side wanted my mother to be buried in their compound with my father. They got angry and there was lots of fighting; the police came. They had to talk, talk, talk. One of my uncles who's a priest brought everything into control. My father's family was still very sad because they wanted my mother to be buried with her husband.

"My uncle, the one who mistreated us, then took us to go live with him again. My other uncle did not ever want us to go back because he knew life there was very, very difficult for us. He knew my uncle just wanted us to work for him day and night for nothing and he knew we were maltreated. Emmanuel's twin sister, Samira, finally complained to my other uncle, who came and got Emmanuel and me. We were thankful to get out of there once and for all. Our nightmare life with that man was about to be over!

"Our good uncle then brought the two of us here to the Good Shepherd Home on 11 September 2003. He had heard from a neighbor that Sister Jane wanted to start an orphanage for children just like us, so he had contacted the Sisters ahead of time and they were happy to take us in. At that time, they had no other children. It was just me and Emmanuel; we were the first. When we came it was a big, big deal because Sister Jane's dream of starting an orphanage was beginning to happen. Then Nafi Ndika came next, then Che Blaise and Franklin." At the mention of his new brothers, Mobiya became animated.

"So the five of us were the first to come to the Good Shepherd Home; we were all boys. Our mother, Sister Jane, was in the United States then, but she knew we were coming because the other Sisters told her. I was very happy when the other boys came to live here; I thought it would be just the two of us. Nafi Ndika came about two months after us, then the others."

"So you had new brothers. What did you think?" I asked, joining in his excitement.

"It was fine; it was fine," he answered, grinning and nodding his head.

"Where are your other brothers and sisters?"

"The other five are learning a trade. They live on their own. One is a seamstress. They are older than me. I don't know where my other sisters and brothers are from the other mother, but my own brothers and sisters do come here to visit us."

We just sat there in silence as I continued to absorb what Mobiya had told me. I had no reference point for a nine-year-old holding his mother closely to his young body while she died, then hiking two hours through rough terrain and fording a rushing river in the middle of the night to tell her family. I had a great deal to learn from these children.

Finally I began, "You must have been so afraid and so sad, Mobiya . . . and now I hear you make very good grades and want to be a doctor. What makes you want to be a doctor?"

"I want to help other children . . . like save lives. I like to say it out loud sometimes," he exclaimed proudly, and off he went down the dirt road to join his brothers and sisters in a game of basketball on the outdoor court of packed earth.

Note

1. All children in Cameroon, both boys and girls, refer to their clothes as dresses.

CHAPTER 10

Claiming My Calling— Again

"**My dear, my dear, you are sick,**" called Sister Jane one morning, rushing into my bedroom.

"I am?" I said groggily, sitting bolt upright in bed. "What's the matter with me?"

"My dear, it is ten o'clock. You are sick!" exclaimed Sister Jane, wearing a printed wrap over her habit.

"Let me get coffee for you. I'll go bring it now," she offered.

"What a wuss I am," I thought. Here she was worried about me oversleeping, while from what I could already tell she only stopped working to sleep, and even then she often took care of infants in the middle of the night. In the United States we are taught to be careful of our boundaries, making sure we take our days off. But Sister Jane had no concept of a day off, much less a vacation. My own commitment to helping others paled in comparison.

I was relieved when Lillian arrived with the coffee instead of Sister Jane. "You know there's no place in the world like this," Lillian mused, as I drank my coffee. "No matter where I've traveled, I have never been to another place like this. Here we actually get to live with people in their own culture, their own space. There's nothing really to compare this to."

It was true. We were so privileged in so many ways; the economic privilege of our lives in the United States was beginning to feel shameful. And yet, I had stayed in luxury hotels and never slept better or felt more at peace than I had here. I had given keynote addresses on hospitality across the United States, yet had never been greeted as warmly and with as much exuberance as I had here. And no matter where I had gone outside my own home, the outpouring of love here was unlike any I had ever experienced. I had much to learn as I tried to unpack these seeming dichotomies, all the while coming to terms with the immense material wealth of my own country and the immense material poverty of theirs.

I thought I had dealt with this. In 1985, I was the thirty-two-year-old wife of a Wall Street investment banker living in Princeton, New Jersey, and something felt out of kilter to me. I had grown up in Tennessee surrounded by economic advantage, but Princeton was altogether something different. I was not accustomed to people with full-time nannies and family trust funds, or Nobel Prize winners and well-known CEOs at the next restaurant table. I was not accustomed to my husband's eighty-hour work week and constant travel, lunch meetings in Europe, dinners in New York, and lavish business entertaining.

Then came an announcement in our daughter Charlotte's kindergarten newsletter about an opportunity to teach at Martin House, a settlement house in the most impoverished part of Trenton, New Jersey, only twenty-five minutes from our home. I left it in a pile of paperwork. Another announcement came. I ignored it again.

Eventually, I had to wonder whether I was supposed to learn something in Trenton. Was it time for me to face my fear of people I didn't even know and fear of what I might find out about myself if I met them? I remembered Martin Luther King Jr., a figure so central to the South and my upbringing. Finally, seventeen years after his assassination, I headed to Martin House and started to march with him.

My perspective on reality changed forever, as I learned uncomfortable truths. And what was the truth? The median income for whites in America at that time was $42,439; for African Americans it was $25,351. The portion of our overall population living in poverty was 12.7 percent, while for African Americans it was an alarming 26.1 percent. The largest percentage of hate crimes in America was and still is against African Americans.

 In the land of opportunity, I quickly learned that there is no such thing as equal opportunity, and that in the midst of our land of plenty there is a permanent underclass. I learned that the triple effects of racism, sexism, and classism are more devastating than I could have imagined. I learned that homeless women have the same hopes and dreams for their children as I have for mine. I learned that motherhood and pain are the universal language.

Before I began working in Trenton, I thought of poverty primarily in Sunday morning sermons or weeknight news reports. On such occasions, my mind filled with masses of hungry, poor people in developing nations, images of people in inner city or rural settings throughout our own country. My feelings of compassion and concern for these nameless people were overshadowed by frustration at my own inability to change anything.

Once I ventured into inner city Trenton, "the poor" could no longer be an abstraction for me. The poor are now Myrtle, Lamar, Emma, Scott, and Resa. I know now that the poor are parents who have hopes and dreams that their children will have a better life. They are men and women with vivid dreams for themselves, and they need help removing systemic barriers that stand between them and their goals.

Images of my African American students those many years ago came back to me on that warm African morning. There was Jennifer who carried all her worldly belongings in a bag and often hummed loudly to block out the voices in her head. There was Beatrice who had been raped repeatedly by her father and who told me one day that Whitney Houston's popular song about "learning to love yourself" had changed her life forever. There was Roseann, terrified that the violence all around her would seep into her life and the lives of her children, preventing them from even growing up.

There was Justina, thin as a rail and addicted to crack cocaine, who just disappeared one day. There was Tyrone who was proud of his uncle because he had gotten his picture on the front page of the newspaper by robbing a bank and shooting an innocent bystander. There was James who played Russian roulette by testing street drugs at random to determine if they were "safe" or had been laced with something deadly. In spite of insurmountable odds, each of these students regularly attended class, studied hard, and fervently wished to break the cycle of poverty in which they found themselves. They were resolute in their determination to change their own lives.[1]

Twenty years later in the midst of a little-known African country, I felt a calling back to where I began. It was time to more fully understand the circumstances leading to the entrapment of many Africans in a never-ending cycle of poverty, a cycle that foreign aid has not changed. The details were out of focus, but I knew it is not enough to send money to Africa, or even to visit and tell people back home about the overwhelming numbers of orphaned children still on the streets. I wanted to learn about the systems and help local leaders make changes that would significantly alter their lives.[2]

It was a morning of revelations. I looked up to hear the sound of children playing outside my window.

"Give it to me, give it to me," I heard, along with laughter and the sound of a ball being kicked.

"Here, go here," another voice called in the midst of the sound of feet shuffling on the packed dirt.

Quickly coming back to reality, I ran outside and found to my delight that Nafi was there. Without prompting, he came up and hugged me, putting his head on my chest. I could feel his heart beating and was glad that we were connecting in so short a time. I took his hand and asked if I could watch the game with him. He made a special place for me to sit next to him on a rock and we sat.

There were fifteen children of all ages and stages of dress, lined up watching a soccer game being played with the ball I had brought Nafi. I was floored by the lack of ownership among the children—all clothes and shoes were shared and worn by anyone whom they fit, and all toys and play items were shared. The white, pearlized leather ball I had brought was already brown with dirt from the morning's play as five of the older boys, wearing flip-flops, expertly kicked it around one of the opposing players and into an imaginary goal.

During the game, Phoebe, one of the caretakers for the children, called Nafi over and began cutting his fingernails with a straight-edged razorblade like the ones used in old Gillette razors. She did it for ten children, all without so much as one nick or drop of blood.

Interruptions past, Nafi joined the game with the older boys, and he really knew what to do with a soccer ball. At least a head shorter than the rest, he was quick and maneuvered the ball well. Now I knew why Sister Jane had suggested this particular gift for him. I hoped that he would have many more such games in the months and years ahead.

When the game ended, Nafi and I walked to his room; he was ready for a break. I then walked up the dirt hill to the computer room just outfitted by Nan and Divine.

"Have you ever worked on computers at school?" I asked Mobiya, who had been one of the first to make a beeline to the room.

"No, I've never had the chance before."

Soon I heard the sound of the Windows operating system launching and decided it might just be one of the new universal sounds.

"I've seen a computer before," added Mobiya, "but we've never had anyone to teach us what to do with them."

"This is called a mouse," Nan told him. "You move it around like this, and when you get where you want to go, you click twice on this side but sometimes you only need to click once. When I say 'click,' I mean you just need to push down." Her patience astounded me.

Eventually, we heard the voice of Mavis Beacon, a typing instructor known all over the world. Mobiya had heard of her and was thrilled with the chance to soak up her lesson. "I never got to do this before. I never got to do this!"

Here was another student, many miles and many years away from those I had taught at Martin House, yet his desire and determination to succeed against all odds mirrored theirs. This young man of fourteen, who had endured profound hardship, was using a computer for the very first time, and his joy could not be contained.

"A S D F," he called as he hit the keys, "W E R T."

Notes

1. Elizabeth Rankin Geitz, *Entertaining Angels* (Harrisburg, PA: Morehouse Publishing, 1993), 102–103.

2. When considering a call to action for aid to Africa, see Dambisa Moyo's *Dead Aid: Why Aid Is Not Working and How There Is a Better Way for Africa*, New York: Farrar, Straus, and Giroux, 2009. Unlike many of the economists who write about Africa, Moyo is African. Her book traces why $1 trillion in aid over the last fifty years has not helped and has actually hurt Africa. The aid to which she refers is primarily large-scale government-to-government aid, which too often fosters corruption among African officials. Non-targeted development aid often falls into the hands of dishonest government officials as well. However, aid geared toward specific self-sufficiency projects and microfinance loans is successful.

See also *White Man's Burden: Why the West's Efforts to Aid the Rest Have Done So Much Ill and So Little Good*, New York: Penguin, 2007, by William Easterly, former research economist at the World Bank. "Without feedback from the poor who need the aid, no one in charge really understands exactly what trouble spots need fixing. True victories against poverty, he demonstrates, are most often achieved through indigenous, ground-level planning." (Publisher's Weekly Review, March 20, 2007)

CHAPTER 11

The Orphans' Plight

As I walked out of the computer room, Father Joseph Ngijoe entered, dressed in a black clergy shirt with stiff, white priest's collar indicating his role as chaplain to the Home. I had been looking forward to speaking with him to get his perspective on the situation in Cameroon, as well as on the Home itself. His face beamed with an infectious I-love-everybody smile when he saw me.

"Elizabeth, I've been looking for you. How are you?" he asked in English with a French accent.

"I've never been better," I responded, smiling from ear to ear myself.

"I have a chair waiting for you," he said eagerly, his white sneakers and white floppy hat gleaming in the sun. "Let's go." And we traveled back to the courtyard where there were two hard-backed chairs, overlooking the valley below with lush, green mountains in the distance rising just above the densely populated city.

After we settled in, he began to share his reflections. "What we can see here at the Home is the love of God materialized, the love that has no boundary. The people of America keep coming and see that they can be part of making life better for the fatherless children, the motherless children who the Sisters are taking care of so they can have a future. Especially we are grateful to Sister Mary Lynne, of the Community of St. John Baptist in New Jersey, who comes here every year for two months to see that the children are being well taken care of. I don't know where we would be without her, and she has encouraged other good people from America to contribute to our work here. It's wonderful to be able to take care of those who are not expecting to live and now these children . . ."

"Do you think these children really would have died?" I asked him.

"Yes."

"Because of lack of food or healthcare or both?"

"Well, all at the same time," he admitted. "The children die from those things right on the streets or in the bush away from prying eyes, not just here but all over Africa. It's horrible to see. Horrible."

As he spoke, I realized it hadn't sunk in yet that most of the children surrounding me, laughing and playing, would be dead if it weren't for the Good Shepherd Home. The children were so alive, so full of life, it was impossible to picture the alternative.

Joseph continued, "But now the children are able to live like they're in a regular home through the love of the Sisters who make sure that at least the children can have good food. Sister Jane is their mother. There is no doubt about that. She loves these children just as if they were her biological children.

"She sees that they get good food, good education, good treatment, and it is not easy. You see, she was attracted here by love, seeing children who were abandoned on the street. A lot could have happened to them except for the love of Sister Jane, and now she has a home for them and the many blessings of a community. Other good people now embrace her vision and are making it their own. For example, now we have a school for the little kids, which is so wonderful.

"Can you imagine there were people in this town who looked at these children differently because they were orphans? They were the rejected ones, even by their teachers. The fact that most of their parents died of AIDS gives them even more of a stigma," he lamented, shaking his head. "They are the face of AIDS in Africa today. These innocent children who are still alive are the suffering silent ones in this great tragedy."

"It seems to me that with so many AIDS orphans here in Africa they wouldn't be mistreated like that," I offered.

"Oh, but they are. You have to understand that some people still think AIDS is caused by witchcraft and that somehow these innocent children have inherited that. They don't want them around their own children; it's why they are so rejected. About forty percent of our population believes in traditional African religion that includes witchcraft and voodoo. So that belief is a definite factor in how these orphans are treated."

"It seems to affect how Sister Jane's treated also. She told us about the man who used witchcraft to try to get her and the Sisters to move, and then about the man who tried to poison her."

"Oh yes; it's definitely a factor. In March 2005, the Catholic University of Central Africa in Yaoundé organized an international conference on witchcraft and social justice. They were trying to get a handle on the actual prevalence of the practice. It was a major news story at the time. Hair-raising, I tell you!

"Now with AIDS, this is a social area in which our government and many other governments in Africa have no plan. People are dying and more and more children are left behind. There are 300,000 orphans in Cameroon alone whose parents have died of AIDS and in all of Africa the last number I heard was 45 million."[1]

"I can't even wrap my mind around a number like that. It's just unbelievable," I sighed. "So how many orphanages are there?"

"In the country as a whole I'm not sure, but here in Bamenda there are only two or three others, and they're not really having any impact. People do not understand that you can take good care of children you do not know. So, instead of going to an orphanage, many orphans stay in the house of extended families and they end up living like slaves. The families use them to do all the work and to bring in money for the rest of the family. There isn't another orphanage like this, and a lot of orphans are dying," he noted.

I was shocked that the government seemed so incapable of intervention, but Joseph was in no way surprised. "That's the policy of the government here," he said. "You know, Cameroon has been a country at peace in Africa for many years. There hasn't been major war, so they're not prepared for something unexpected like this current crisis. There is nothing, absolutely nothing the government has put aside to care for this number of children. I think one of the things Sister did is go to the governor and invite him to visit the orphanage so he can see what is happening and really understand."

"So did the governor come?"

"Yes. The wife of the governor has come here."

"But did the governor come?"

"No, he sent delegates. The visitors came here to the Home and some of them were very shocked. They didn't realize how an institution like this works. There was a time when people like Sister Jane were very helpful to the government. You see, with a child who is homeless the government would say, 'Ah, the Sister has an orphanage. Let's take the child there.' So the Social Affairs people would bring the child here and that would be it.

"Then they would leave, because they would say the Sister is taking care of it. They had no understanding of what was needed for these children to survive, no sense of the day-to-day struggle. In the three years I've been here, the Good Shepherd Home has received no funds from the government—none. But just recently we did receive some food and goods from the Chantal Biya Foundation, run by President Biya's wife. That's been very helpful to us.

"Americans provide the bulk of our support, but fortunately some of the local churches are reaching out to us now. So we do have Africans helping Africans and that's very important. Even so, most of the people here don't know much about this orphanage," he said, shaking his head. "Because of their culture some people think this is nonsense. They don't think it's normal to keep someone else's children. They don't realize that there are so many orphans, that there's a real crisis in our country. The newspapers have sometimes written about events here, but most of the people just don't understand.

"And the fact that Sister Jane is a woman is also a factor. People aren't used to women being in charge. Sister Jane's a real firestorm, and some people just don't know what to think about that. They think it's unnatural. Women should have the babies and wait on the men, do what they say, you know.

"In African culture, women are always looked on as second class and they are not," Joseph continued. "Here at Good Shepherd we want to change that. When people look at the way our culture is and then can see that in the Bible women are accepted by God . . . well, that can be useful for many good things."

We sat in silence looking out over the beautiful lush valley below, absorbed in thought. Finally, I ventured into new territory.

"There's something else I've wanted to talk with you about. I was thinking about the children before I came here and the fact that most of their parents died of AIDS. I decided to do some research on the AIDS pandemic in Africa and as you might guess, there was a lot about homosexuality. I read about the way they're treated in your country and began to wonder if there was some connection between prejudice against homosexuals, prejudice against people with AIDS, and prejudice against the orphans."

"Elizabeth, I would say you're on to something there," he noted with a sly grin.

"So I'm curious," I continued, emboldened by his response. "How are homosexuals treated here in Cameroon?"

I was well aware of the trouble the Episcopal Church in the United States was having at that time with Cameroon's next-door neighbor, Nigeria. When the Episcopal Church consecrated Gene Robinson as the first openly gay bishop in the world-wide Anglican Communion, it inspired Nigerian Archbishop Peter Akinola to lead a protest that threatens to split the Anglican Communion. He remains convinced that Robinson's consecration is against the teachings of scripture and wants nothing to do with the Episcopal Church, not even accepting Episcopal money for the many social needs of his country.

"Ah, but you see, they do not view it as you do," Joseph explained. "They do not see it as justice or no justice. They see it as a sexual issue, an immorality, an abomination."

I reminded him that, in some African countries like Somalia, people who happen to be gay can be sentenced to death. In Cameroon, they can be sent to jail.[2] Joseph took all this into account and offered his own insights.

"The prejudice here in Cameroon against gays is high—ninety-two percent of our people condemn them," he said. "That has increased the difficulties faced by our National AIDS Committee in providing outreach both in terms of prevention as well as support for those who are HIV positive. It takes a long time for someone to admit to being gay because it's against the law. . . . The truth is this is a subject we do not discuss here; it's outlawed and people are afraid to even talk about it."

"I read about a case where eleven men were recently jailed in Cameroon," I said, "but the papers didn't comment one way or the other on how they were treated.[3] Do you work to try to get the laws changed?"

"No, here at the Good Shepherd Home all of our work is for the children. But that doesn't mean we don't have love in our hearts for gay people. Sister Jane has good friends who are gay. She loves them very much, and I do, too, because they are God's children. But we don't have the luxury [of becoming advocates for gay rights].

You see, we're trying just to survive day in and day out . . . but if someone else were to work for this, yes. It would help! I mean, why would anyone submit to AIDS treatment when they know they can be accused of being gay and end up in jail? That's why so much of it goes untreated and people end up dying, like the parents of many of our children here." Joseph sounded weary.

"It's all connected isn't it?" I finally asked. "Oh yes," he assured me, "it's all connected."

Notes

1. "According to the latest statistics released by the United Nations Children's Fund (UNICEF) and the Joint United Nations Programme on HIV/AIDS (UNAIDS), there are 48.3 million orphans south of the Sahara desert, one-quarter of whom have lost their parents to AIDS. . . . Projections by the two U.N. agencies suggest that by 2010, there would be 53.1 million children under eighteen bereft of their parents, 15.7 million of whom will have had parents who died of AIDS." See *http://ipsnews.net/news.asp?idnews=35827*; "Africa: A Continent of Orphans" by Mario de Queiroz, December 13, 2006.

2. "In March of 2009, eight months after this conversation took place, the National Assembly of Cameroon voted in favor of a law authorizing President Biya to ratify the Maputo Protocol on Human Rights and the Rights of Women. It was widely reported in the African press (see [*AfricaNews.com*, posted 5 July 2009]), that the Protocol legalized same-sex marriage in Cameroon. It did not. The Protocol never once mentions the word 'homosexual', nor refers to it in any way. Alternatives-Cameroun put out a press release on 6 July 2009 stating clearly that same-sex practice is still criminalized in Cameroon, citing deliberate manipulations of the Catholic Church in Douala to avoid the ratification of the Maputo Protocol. The Maputo Protocol is a comprehensive document giving full and equal rights to women and outlawing female circumcision. Article 14 of the document also legalizes abortion under certain circumstances. To sway public opinion against the Protocol, false allegations were made linking it to the legalization of homosexuality." (E-mail received August 19, 2010 from Steave Nemande, M.D., Chair, Alternatives-Cameroun)

3. "Since 2005, Alternatives-Cameroun, Human Rights Watch, and other Cameroonian and international organizations have documented abuses and violence against LGBT people in Cameroon," Human Rights Watch said in an August 19, 2010 media release. "Suspected homosexual men have been arrested and beaten on their bodies, heads, and even the soles of their feet while in custody. Women suffer violence in their families if they are suspected of being lesbians. In some cases, they have been forced to leave their homes, or their children have been taken away from them."

CHAPTER 12

Clemence Kalla

Clemence had heard about my talk with Mobiya and was ready for her turn. "Let's go inside," she said motioning to me without hesitation, clearly prepared. We walked inside and sat on the cushioned sofas and chairs trimmed in wood.

She began with no prompting. "I'm sixteen years old and my life here is wonderful. I've been here four years, and the place is lovely," Clemence shared in a soft, almost lyrical voice. Like all children in the Home, her head was shaved to ward off lice, but it had grown back just enough to look stylish. With big gold loop earrings and a blue and white shirt, Clemence was a beautiful young lady, poised and thoughtful.

"My parents died when I was still a little girl. My dad died first and later my mother died, so I went to live with my uncle. Life there was not easy. His wife never loved me; she was really hard on me, very hard. She had two daughters and we all got up in the morning together, but I had to do all the work. I had to wash the plates and mop the floors. When I went to school I was always late, so I was beaten at school every day.

"My aunt ended up not allowing me to go to school at all. I was more intelligent than her daughter, and she was jealous. She was always complaining there was no money for my fees, so I was forced to leave school. I had to work all day in the house and yard, moving furniture to clean, bringing heavy logs inside for the fire. I had to walk two hours to the market and then carry all the food home by myself. Sometimes I was so tired, I thought I would collapse, but she didn't care, and I was forced to keep working," she continued in a voice that, like Mobiya's, was surprisingly devoid of emotion.

"When my aunt fed us each night, she had a big bamboo tray. She fed us from that. Even though we were still very hungry and not satisfied after the food we'd eaten, it was all gone so she told us to go outside and play. She then called for her own children to come back in and she would add more food to the tray for them to eat. That's how they were doing every day, but I never knew what was going on. There I was working hard all day long and not being fed hardly anything to eat. I was becoming thinner and thinner.

"One day we were playing outside with another friend and that friend had to leave early. I rushed into the house to get water to drink. That's when I found the two children eating. As if I couldn't figure out what they were doing, they said, 'Oh, Clemence, where have you been? We have been looking for you! Come eat; we have some more food.' I realized that's what had been happening every day, so I got angry and started crying. I refused to eat. I left, and was crying out as loud as I could in the road. I couldn't stop; my body was racked with sobs.

"One lady heard me and asked what was the matter," she said. "She was from the Bafut tribe like me. I told her what had been happening as best I could in the state I was in, so she went to the village and told my grandpa how I was being maltreated by my uncle. My grandfather said, 'They should not be treating Clemence that way. They should send her back to the village to be with me. Get her out of there!' So my grandfather took me, but he was really old. I was nine and I was forced to take care of him."

"Life in the interior part of Bafut where he lived is very hard. There was nothing for my grandfather to do. He was too old to work on a farm. When he got up in the morning he just went to a palm tree to see if he could get some palm wine, some white stuff we call it.[1] He sat there the whole day, drinking and discussing. That's all he did. He was about eighty years old. My other aunt who lived somewhere else would, at times, bring us food. Otherwise we had nothing to eat. My uncle, her husband, finally brought me here to the Good Shepherd family where I could find shelter and enough to eat. My uncle was a friend of Uncle Laurence who works here at the Home. It was through him that I came here."

Sister Jane walked up, free from her duties and ready to join in sharing the story. "Uncle Laurence told me he had heard there was a girl called Clemence living with her grandfather somewhere far in the bush and that the child was not going to school and it was really hard for her. I said, 'Bring her to us. Get her to us to help her.' I kept on asking where she was. But nothing happened. The uncle was not willing to help the child. So I kept on pushing, pushing, pushing. Finally the uncle brought her here and when she arrived you should have seen her. She was thin from lack of food and full of despair. We soon discovered how bright she was. So I said, 'Okay, instead of going to Form One, let's put her in Form Two.[2] And now, she is aspiring to be a medical doctor. It will happen. She can do it."

Turning to Clemence, I asked what it was like when she arrived at the Home.

"I had never thought I would one day be happy again, because I was always sad," she recalled. "It was really hard for me to see my mates all going to school when I wasn't allowed to go. I had been put up and then put up another grade because they knew I could do the work. They knew I could cope. I was very young when I finished Primary School; then nothing. No school. I really cried a lot. I wanted my education, but it was being denied to me. Even in the midst of my tears, I still had to work hard all day in the hot sun outside and then indoors the heat of the iron almost melted me. Without enough food to eat it was awful. All the tears were over when I found the Good Shepherd Home. I never thought I would be what I am today. Everything is just going the way I want now.

"I get up in the morning at five o'clock and say my prayers. Then I concentrate on my morning duty. I do the laundry for the babies, then go to school. I walk with friends to get there. I'm in Secondary School now and will graduate in three years. I walk to the Home after school. We eat and then we have fifty minutes to rest. I then get water from the kitchen for the babies and warm it on the fire. I put it in a big bowl and dilute it with cold water so it will be normal temperature. We bathe sixteen babies at the end of each day. After we bathe them, other girls dress them for bed.

"Oh," she said, as if suddenly remembering, "I want to give you something. Is it okay if I give you a prayer I wrote? It's mostly about the feelings I had before I came here and what I hope will happen in my country."

She handed me a well-worn, folded piece of paper, which I asked her to read aloud. With no hesitation, she began:

CLEMENCE'S PRAYER

To you, O Lord, I offer my prayers.
Give strength to all the lawyers.
Let them be able to defend my rights;
Let it be possible for me to see light.
Give more wisdom to our leaders.
Save me from this situation.
In your constant love and forgiveness remember me.
Let my troubles be stricken away by these leaders.
Let action be taken by these leaders.

I depend on you at all times.
So, Lord, take this poverty away.
I have no biological mother, father or relative.
I am an orphan, ill, unhappy and inactive.
Let there be equality, no wars, no hunger and no
    bad economy.
Let there be world peace, no orphans, enough school,
    no enemies.
Take away AIDS, and let there be affordable drugs for all.
Provide me with what I need.
Let there be no selfish leaders, bad leaders.
Drop all the bad ones.

Give a little orphan girl like me courage to grow up to be
    a strong woman.
Eradicate the gender discrimination that most of my people
    have toward women.
Be merciful to me Lord for I am lonely and weak.
Do not let anybody who is willing to help me and my friends
    be weak.
Give them strength.
Give me strength.

Give more strength to our mother, Sister Jane of this
    Good Shepherd Home Orphanage.

Give strength to all the workers of the Good Shepherd
    Home Orphanage.
Give more energy, power and wisdom to our mothers, aunts,
    and uncles in the United States.
I pray for more blessings to those nice people in the United
    States who are helping us.

I pray for you. And you.
I pray for the leaders in this country.
I pray for the leaders in all countries.
Amen.[3]

Notes

1. Palm wine is a popular drink in parts of Africa made from the sap collected from a palm tree, much like maple syrup is collected. The white liquid that initially collects tends to be cold and have an intoxicating effect. As it ferments, it becomes increasingly alcoholic. Local tradition holds that palm wine increases sperm production in men and breast-milk in lactating mothers.

2. Grade levels in Cameroon are: Nursery; Primary School—Class 1–6; Secondary School or College—Form 1–5; High School—1st and 2nd Cycle; University.

3. Clemence's Prayer was later published as "An Orphan's Prayer" in Margaret Rose and Jenny Te Paa, et al., editors, *Lifting Women's Voices: Prayers to Change the World* (New York: Morehouse Publishing, 2009), 5–6. It has been edited for inclusion here.

CHAPTER 13

Mother Teresa of Africa

Sister Jane never had the luxury of a break. One afternoon a woman in dire need arrived at the Home. She was in the main room with her eldest daughter, just outside our eating area, when we walked in for dinner. I had thought Sister Jane only helped children; I was wrong.

"So they just dropped in and you didn't know who they were?" I asked when we were safely out of the woman's hearing.

Sister Jane nodded affirmatively. "You know, we feed about sixty people each week like this. It's just . . . sometimes it's just . . . I don't know." She shook her head. "She told me that she has been to a doctor. A man came and got married to her. They had that first child. The man then left."

"We wish you a Merry Christmas. We wish you a Merry Christmas," her cell phone chimed.

"Hallo? Hallo? I cannot hear you," she said. Click.

"So I am telling you . . ."

"We wish you a Merry Christmas; we wish you a Merry Christmas," it rang once more.

"Hallo? Hallo? What? I cannot hear you. . . . No, I do not have the money to send to your son in prison . . . no . . . we cannot get news. Do not call back, okay? . . . Thank you." Click.

"What was all that about?" I asked curiously.

"One of the orphan's uncles got put in prison, and they want me to get him out."

"So why is he in prison?" Lillian asked.

"I don't know all the details, but somebody accused him of raping somebody. Unfortunately many people here do not think that's such a big deal," Sister Jane replied, shaking her head, obviously upset.

I was trying to absorb this surprising information when she continued telling us her visitor's plight. "So that woman sitting out there came with a big story. When she was pregnant with twins, one of whom is the child sitting with her now, the father abandoned her. Then when the twins were a year old, he came back and told her, 'You know, I will take care of you,' so she took him back. And then he got her pregnant again. He left. She had twins the second time. The third time, he came again and said, 'You know, I will really try my best this time.' She accepted. Twins again. And then he left just when the pregnancy was there; and then another man came who promised her the same thing and she accepted. Twins came. And then that man went. He came again."

We groaned. This story was clearly not getting any better.

"And now," Sister Jane continued in a hushed voice, so as not to be overheard, "she is pregnant with twins again. The second man promised that this time he would not leave her. That this time things would be different."

"What does she want you to do?" Lillian asked.

"Well, she is coming to tell me that there is no way for her to go to the hospital. If she starts laboring now there is no way; she has nothing. The children she has are sleeping on the floor. You know, with all those children she's not eating well. You see how she is."

I had seen how she was when I passed her on the way in. Even though she was very pregnant; her legs, arms and upper body looked thin, her face gaunt. The child sitting next to her was too thin also. As she sat on Sister Jane's couch in a moo-moo made of local printed fabric, the bright colors did not hide her obvious need.

In an attempt to find some focus, Lillian asked, "Sister Jane, are you familiar with the term 'mission statement'? All non-profits in America have them. It states your purpose for existing. If you had a mission statement that defines exactly who you are and what you can and cannot do, maybe it would help. You could say that your focus is just on the children."

"The only thing is, sometimes people die," Sister Jane replied clearly.

"I know, your heart gets involved in it. I know, but you can't save the world!"

"That's true," Sister Jane agreed. "But this woman needs help. What they are asking for is not even something to eat. It's that if she starts to labor, for her it will be terrible. In the hospital if you don't have the necessary things, they will not accept you. They need gloves from you, all the things."

"Oh, you have to provide that?" Lillian said, obviously taken aback.

"Yes," Sister Jane said. "I buy them from the pharmacy and give them to the mothers. I have taken a woman in labor to the hospital before and if one item is missing from the kit—one item—they will not take her because they are risking their lives with HIV. Many of the nurses are afraid."

Someone called for Sister Jane. "I'll be right there," she answered, heading into the other room to take care of the woman who had come seeking help.

After she left, I suggested to Lillian and Nan that perhaps we could buy supplies for the kits and put them together for the women. Neither of them agreed, as they felt it would attract an entirely different group of people with different needs. Nan was clear that our focus needed to be on obtaining funds for completing the dormitory, and staying on task was key. Realizing that we were dealing with a Mother Teresa who could never turn someone in genuine need away, we began to strategize among ourselves.

When Sister Jane came back into the room, I turned to a more practical issue. "Sister Jane, how can anyone have four sets of twins? Do you think this woman is telling you the truth?"

"Yes, I know someone who saw her condition where she is living now. They sent her here."

As gently as possible, my friends and I probed more around the likelihood that one woman could bear so many sets of twins.

Sister Jane pushed our doubts aside. "My dear we have had people in Bafut who have had twins six times. I know them. I went to school with some of their children. They pair up, they pair up, they pair up."

She turned her attention to the young woman, completely committed to her need. "I told her when she's in labor she should go to a certain doctor. She's eight months pregnant. Now she's telling me that the doctor asked her to bring thirty thousand francs when she is coming. That's about $80. So if that can save her life . . ."

Having resolved the matter, she turned yet again and began to sing to little Esther, one of the newest babies in the home. "Es, Es, Es, Es, Es," Sister Jane cooed in a singsong voice, looking very much at peace in the midst of the turmoil around her.

I wondered about the orphans in the Home, a number of whose mothers had died in childbirth. I wondered if they had been denied admission to a hospital due to the lack of an $80 kit.

Mission statements? What does a mission statement matter when a person's life hangs in the balance? And where was the government? Sister Jane should never have been forced to decide whether to spend $80 to buy this woman's sterile hospital kit or to buy food for the orphans in her care. She has the heart and call of a Mother Teresa, enough compassion and love for every single person who walks in her door, but how much could one person deal with day after day?

Over dinner, Lillian picked up the thread. "Do you get a lot of information from your brother confirming these situations and telling you which doctors to use?" she asked, knowing Sister Jane's brother is a medical doctor.

"His place of work is too far from here; they sent him into the bush—far, far, far away."

"Who sent him to the bush?" I asked.

"The government. My brother is looking for a way to get out of this country. He doesn't want to stay here. He has worked so hard. Before he went to work in the hospital, it was a terrible place. There was no place for women to put to birth; there was no maternity; there was not a surgery place," Sister Jane informed us before lifting Esther high above her lap again. "Es, Es, Es . . . ," she cooed.

"So my brother worked hard," she continued. "But because he didn't want to give bribes to the minister in charge of hospitals, they gave him a demotion. They sent him to the bush, and he is not there with his wife or children. There is no school, so they stayed behind. There is nothing. My brother has no electricity, and his life is at risk in that place. The place is far in the bush. It is terrible!

"People believe he has money, so they think they can attack him," she said, clearly upset. "Instead of bringing him to the provincial where the people wanted him (because they say that wherever he goes he always makes the place better), they sent him to the bush. So when he left where he was, people marched in the streets. People wanted him back. People even from here will go out to the bush to see him."

"Sister Jane, when you say 'out in the bush', where is that?" I asked.

"It's not near a city. It's in a very rural area, out where you fend for yourself," Lillian explained.

"Where people have to travel long ways and the roads . . . they are terrible roads and people use horses to travel; life there is not easy," Sister Jane added, shaking her head.

"What kind of doctor is he? Does he do surgery?"

"He does. He does all," she replied, obviously proud of her brother. "Women come to him when they have growths; they say he knows what he's doing."

"Like a tumor."

"Yes. He's very special with that."

"How long has he been out there?" Lillian asked.

"It's getting to two years now. It's terrible. He says he will resign."

It was apparent that feeding, clothing, and sheltering the children were only a small part of Sister Jane's struggles. I was grateful to sit at her feet and listen.

"Oh," she said, suddenly brightening. "Would you like to see the YouTube video of the Cameroon bottle dance?"

"Sure!" we all replied, ready for a break from the heavy conversation. Once everyone had settled around the computer and it finally booted up, she went to YouTube, typed in "Cameroon bottle dance," and a music video popped on. Immediately Sister Jane was on her feet dancing. "Come on, Mama Lizzie, you'll like this. Watch!" I did and there on the screen, in full African dress, were women and men doing what I would call a combination of the jitterbug and the electric slide. On and on they danced, as Sister Jane swirled around the room with a mock partner, her nun's habit flowing, hips swaying, feet moving. Soon Lillian, Nan, and I joined her as we attempted to mimic the dancers on the screen. Clearly, everyone needed this release. As the video ended, our impromptu dance came to an end and it was time to head back to our rooms.

We said our good nights, picked up our torches, and walked with the two security guards back to our guest quarters with the iron door and barred windows.

As we rounded the corner, I heard the sweet sound of children clapping, singing, and praying, their young voices soaring into the dark, damp night air.

CHAPTER 14

Dancing around Sex

Since the moment she arrived, Nan had been drawn to an infant boy named Issa Zanga. I often found her rocking him and giving him a bottle. One day, she asked Sister Jane, "Can you tell me Issa's story?"

"The mother of Issa is alive, a very young woman. Her parents sent her to school and she had a pregnancy with a young boy, so they rented a small place. When she gave birth to her first child, after four or five months, she took him again. She got pregnant again, and she told me that she would have aborted the baby but she persevered. She told me she didn't want the child and was going to dump the baby. The boy who she had the child with left her."

"Do people here ever have abortions?" asked Lillian.

"Yes, women abort children and the women die. It is not legal and many people die trying to have one. If you are known as a doctor who makes abortion happen, you are known as a very terrible person because of the danger involved."[1]

"The doctor she went to see encouraged her to give birth. When the child was just one month, she came here. Her first child was still nursing when the second one was born. She sat outside, and she was crying and crying, 'Please, Sister I know you take orphans but take this baby. If you do not take this baby, I promise you I will not be able. This child's life will not be safe.' She cried, 'I love this child, Sister, but I cannot keep him.'

"One day she called and said, 'Mama, I want to ask how Issa is.' I said, 'Issa is fine.' She said, 'Tell him that I love him and when he grows up he'll understand why I did what I did.' So the child will stay in the orphanage and grow up."

I asked Sister Jane about the availability of birth control pills in Africa, and other forms of contraception. She explained they are available, but that most women either cannot afford them or cannot get to a hospital to purchase them. She informed us that only one in five African women use modern birth control.[2]

"It's lack of money and the men. They control women where sex is concerned. That's what I am told by the women who come here. It's a very serious issue."

"Are you teaching the children about sex?" Lillian queried.

"Yes, but when I start talking to them about sex, they start laughing. They think who am I, who knows . . . what? What do I know, a nun? So I get a married woman to talk to them. And they know what their parents died of."

"Sister Jane, I was thinking about this when we were in the room where the teenage boys live. I mean, they're teenage boys and you have teenage girls here," I noted.

"They are brothers and sisters really. They don't have that. We cannot allow sex among the children. It would be a huge problem for us," Sister Jane responded, becoming noticeably agitated.

"Sister Jane, it's wonderful that the children are all like brothers and sisters, but of course they won't always be here on the compound. A number are getting older and will soon leave for university or other locations. Are they being taught how not to contract AIDS?" I asked.

"Oh yes, they know that sex before marriage is wrong."

"Well, wrong or right, many of them are going to have sex before marriage. That's a given. Are they being taught to use condoms if they do have sex?" I asked.

"But the Church is against that and condoms break."

"Sister Jane, the Catholic Church is against condoms and all forms of birth control, but the Anglican Church is not. Our church would never counsel against using condoms to prevent the transmission of the AIDS virus."

"Well, yes . . . Anglicans are liberal about that."

"Yes, we are, and thank God for it," I said, aware of our cultural differences and of Sister Jane's early religious training, but convinced her street smarts would eventually prevail. "Sister Jane, these children's parents died of AIDS. You don't want to take care of them their whole life, and then have them contract AIDS when they leave here."

"No, that would be awful, just awful," she replied. "But I don't know. I mean you are talking to a nun here."

"Sister Jane, you know Jesus told us to be wise as serpents and innocent as doves. You've got to be wise as a serpent about AIDS. You can't take any chance whatsoever that these children will not know how to protect themselves when the time comes that they are having sex, if they aren't already."

"But you know, they are taught that in school. They teach them all about the reproductive system and HIV/AIDS, everything."

"But Sister Jane, they need to know that *you* approve," I retorted. "They look up to you. They follow what they believe you want for them. They need to know that condoms are a 99 percent protection against contracting the AIDS virus. Abstinence is 100 percent, but condoms are 99 percent."

"Okay, okay." Sister Jane was listening intently, nodding in agreement.

Knowing it wasn't my place to keep pushing, I asked, "How about getting Laurence to talk to the boys?"

"Yes, that would work. He has a girlfriend; they would listen to Laurence."

"Whew," I said, letting out a big breath of air. "Okay, Sister Jane, good."

"It's really surprising you've never had any instances of sexual exploration among the children here," commented Lillian, rejoining the conversation at last.

Sister Jane admitted that they had some problems, first with a driver who got "friendly" with one of the girls; then with a young woman who was working at the Home and brought her boyfriend to stay in her room. But they had dodged the major bullets, especially around sex.

It had always been enough. I was convinced it wouldn't always be.

Notes

1. May 28, 2009, ten months after this conversation took place, President Paul Biya of Cameroon signed the Maputo Protocol for the Human Rights of Women which, in part, legalized abortion. See *www.achpr.org*.

2. Sister Jane's statistics are supported by the 2010 International Planned Parenthood Federation Report, "U.S. Plays a Role in Africa's Birth Control Challenges," *http://www.ippf.org/en/News/Intl+news/US+plays+a+role+in+Africas +birth+control+challenge.htm*. The report states, "Under President George W. Bush, the United States withdrew from its decades-long role as a global leader in supporting family planning, driven by an approach that favored abstinence and shied away from providing contraceptive devices in developing countries, even to married women."

CHAPTER 15

Carine Maru

Shortly before I left America, one of my husband's friends asked what I felt would be the greatest danger to me in Africa. I'm sure he expected me to be concerned about safety issues. Instead, I replied: "Spiritual danger."

He was taken off guard. "You mean you will wonder how God could let something like this happen?" he asked.

"No," I replied, "I'm concerned that I will wonder how *we* could let it happen."

That was one spiritual challenge. Another was seeing how much more deeply spiritual the children and adults in Cameroon seemed to be, compared to me and almost everyone I know in America. It was humbling and chastening to witness the deep and abiding faith of so many people, living it and breathing it every moment of every day. I especially saw that faith alive in Carine.

Like Mobiya and Clemence, Carine shared her story of severe hardship and loss with a neutral face, out of synch with the horror of her story. This is not unusual for people in war-torn or disease-ridden countries; it's part of their survival mechanism. It does not mean, however, that deep wounds and pain do not still exist.[1]

"I lost my father when I was ten; then my mother died that same year," eighteen-year-old Carine began. She was tall and slim, her beautiful ebony skin glowing in the sun. "My father was a farmer and my mother was a primary school teacher. They had five children, one boy and four girls. They both died in the year 2000 when I was ten years. My father died at home and my mother died in the hospital with a fever. She was sick there for eight months.

"After our parents died I felt so sad. All the time I was just crying, crying. My mother always took care of me; that's what made me cry. When my parents died, I became very sick. I could not move at all, so my elder sister had to carry me all the time. They took me to the hospital and while I was there, a nurse cut three of my toes off by accident. They were just removing puss, but they ended up cutting off my toes! It was so painful."

"Then I went home and my father's brother tried to sponsor me in school by paying my fees. I was able to finish Class Six, and then all of a sudden he told me he'd tried his best but was through. He wasn't going to do anything else for me. I don't know why he said this. I stayed in the house three more years working for him and not going to school.

"My uncle had four children who all went to school while I was forced to clean, work on the farm, and take care of everybody. It was so hard! I guess it was because with his four children he could not afford it. I don't know. He never said. But I tell you I was miserable. I was treated like a slave by the people I thought were my family. I thought they would take care of me and they didn't. The children did not treat me like family either. They acted like I worked for them too. It was a nightmare that I thought would never end.

"When my older sister discovered I wasn't allowed to go to school, she told Sister Mary Ann in Bafut, who told Sister Jane. When I came here to the Good Shepherd Home, I really found a lovely mother. Mama Jane is so caring; she shows the same love my parents were showing me. At first she sent me to work in town doing tailoring. I didn't like it, so she sent me back to school. I'm now finally in secondary school.

"Here we're just like a family. We love one another and all the children call me Sister Carine. We care for one another. I cook for the children during the holidays. I also wash their dresses before school. Four of us do the laundry for twenty-one children and then we get to go to school. In the evening we bathe the babies.

"I do this with Clemence. She's my best friend here. She's from the Bafut tribe and I am from the Bassa tribe. My people are from the Western Province in the grasslands. Our villages are very primitive, just like they were centuries ago. Bafut is about an hour from here in the Northwest Province and is more advanced. Anyway, here at Good Shepherd, we get to all live together."

"Yes," I recalled, "Sister Jane told us that it was part of her mission to bring together children from different tribes to live as brother and sister."

"That's right. 'May We All Be One' is our motto, and you know what? We are. I see that now. I didn't understand that at first, but now I do. Every night now I sleep with two children in my bed—Faith and Perpetua. They are one year. Sometimes they climb all over each other but I make sure they are fine. We get up together at 5:00 a.m. and go to bed at 9:00 p.m.

"It's better than sleeping on the floor like I did at my uncle's, and here we are all just happy around. We are sisters and brothers, and we all care for each other. We pray together too. It's a real comfort."

I smiled and nodded my head. The change in her countenance as she talked about her new family was heartening to see. "What are you studying in school, Carine?"

"I want to study marketing and accounting. I want to be in business," she replied, smiling from ear to ear.

Note

1. "Human beings, especially children, have the capacity to repress those experiences or feelings that their conscious life cannot tolerate. Repression means that it is not available to be accessed by ordinary discourse. Not everything that is repressed *should* come to light. Sometimes it is best to 'let sleeping dogs lie.' But there is a caveat; the American form of psychology is not universally relevant. For instance, Sigmund Freud was clear that his psychological system was in reference to a Western European culture. What we should appreciate in each of the children at the Good Shepherd Home is their incredible strength in having survived their horrific life circumstances. I believe it is our job to honor and nurture those strengths." (Interview with Dr. Albert Waldman, psychiatrist and sponsor of one of the orphans, fifteen-year-old Kajethan.)

Sister Jane Mankaa, visionary founder of the Good Shepherd Home for Children and Mother Superior of the Sisters of Bethany in Bamenda, Cameroon.

Mangu Maru carrying a cooking pot to the outdoor
fire pit in preparation for a meal of beans and potatoes.

Abena Mboma drying soybeans on a sunny Cameroonian day.

Cyrille Kwetche laying palm branches on newly
planted crops to protect them during the rainy season.

Mballa Zango carrying the pot she's just washed to the outdoor firepit.

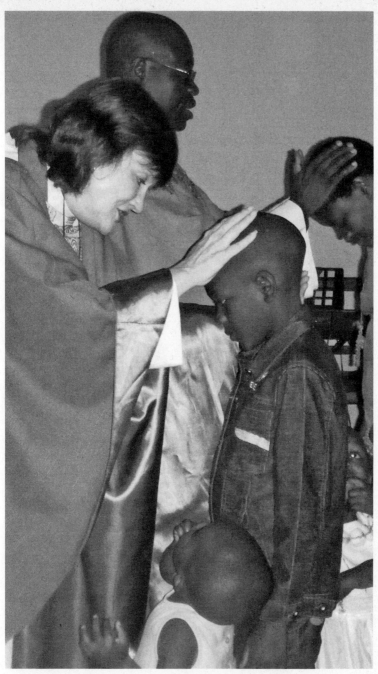

The Rev. Canon Elizabeth Geitz blessing Nafi Ndika as
Father Joseph Ngijoe blesses Mobiya Dbango.

Mobiya Dbango using a computer for the first time, aided by Nan Curtis.

Elizabeth Geitz with Sister Jane Mankaa,
leaving the museum at the palace of the Fon of Bafut.

Lillian Cochran and Franck Banni taking
a walk on the travelers' last afternoon at the Home.

PART III

Deepening Awareness

"If we could change ourselves, the tendencies in the world would also change. . . . We need not wait to see what others do."

—Mahatma Gandhi

"You tell those who have been marginalized and treated as if they do not count, that they matter, that nothing anybody else does to them can alter the most fundamental fact about them. That God loves them . . ."

—Desmond Tutu

CHAPTER 16

Of Railroads and Quilts

One afternoon, I came to Sister Jane wondering about a common theme in too many of the children's stories. "It's very disheartening to learn how many of them have families who treated them like slaves," I observed.

"Yes, it is," she agreed. "A big part of my job is saving children from being slaves within their own families. We help them escape the maltreatment. You know, the way the slaves in America escaped through the Underground Railroad during the Civil War? Well, I see the Good Shepherd Home as like that for our children. It's different because this is above ground in plain sight, but the effect is similar. We're helping the children get out of those situations. If we weren't here, they would have no way out."

Shifting gears, she asked, "Do you all know much about the Underground Railroad?"

"Would you believe my great-great-great uncle ran one of the most famous ones?" I offered. "His name was John Rankin. In fact, his story is told in a book called *Uncle Tom's Cabin*, which is a fictionalized account of the Rankin family saving a slave named Eliza. She escaped slavery in Kentucky with her young son by running over chunks of ice in the Ohio River. The real-life Eliza escaped over ice floes, but then she ran to the safe house of an Underground Railroad on the other side that was owned by my ancestor, the Reverend John Rankin. That part was not in the book.

"The truth is even better than the famous story told in that book. The real-life Eliza, with her son in her arms, crossed the first time over the ice floes, but then she risked going back into Kentucky to get her other five children. On that second trip back, she was being chased by slave hunters, so one of my great-great-great boy cousins dressed as a slave woman. He zigzagged through the woods and made the slave catchers think he was Eliza. They chased him for hours. Meanwhile, Eliza was able to cross the river to the Rankin house. The ice floes were gone by then so a helper of the family guided her and her five children back to safety."

"Wouldn't that son have really been in danger if they'd caught him?" asked Sister Jane, intent on the story.

"Absolutely. Dogs were chasing him and the slave catchers with guns were right behind them.[1] He could have been shot, or if he'd been captured he could have been fined as much as $500 and sent to prison for a year.[2] I was never aware of this until about ten years ago when my brother saw the story in a children's history book. We could hardly believe it. Then we double-checked our family tree and there he was. You see, I was a Rankin before I got married."[3]

"Oh my dear, I am so happy to know that one of your grand-uncles helped start the Underground Railway and that he was also a reverend! He should be smiling on you from heaven to see what you are doing for the poor today," Sister Jane insisted.

"Are there any other stories about him?" she asked with obvious excitement. We all got cups of steaming hot tea and proceeded into the large sitting area of the Home. Once we were settled into the overstuffed chairs, I continued.

"Well, it's not as famous as the one about Eliza, but there's another story about a runaway slave named Tice, who hid in the woods and on nearby plantations. He finally made it to the Ohio River across from the Rankin home in Ripley, Ohio, just like Eliza. He didn't have a boat and there was no ice when he escaped, so he had to dive into the cold water. The man who owned him then followed him in a small boat.

"Tice would have heard one of the sounds commonly used to alert slaves, a certain kind of bird call or the ringing of a bell, for example, that let him know there was someone there to help him on the other side of the river if he could make it across," I explained. "It was recorded by a man named Siebert, who wrote about the system used by the Rankins and the other abolitionists who were their neighbors. It was all designed to help guide the runaways safely to shore. In addition to the bird calls and bells, the Rankins apparently used a light in their attic. Their house sat on a tall bluff overlooking the river. This light was legendary and became a beacon of hope and a visual guide for many miles out on dark nights.

"As the story goes, Tice saw the Rankin light on the bluff and then swam underwater to it, baffling the slaveholder in the skiff who reported that Tice 'just disappeared into something like an underground railroad.' And that, as the story goes, is how it all got its name.[4]

"I don't think of this that often because I never knew John Rankin. But of course I'm very proud of him; his story really gives me something to think about now."

"Well, my family tree is in my head," Sister Jane said, offering us another glimpse into her background. "Our tradition here in Africa is oral. We've learned it all through hearing stories from our grandmothers and their mothers before them."

"Have you ever heard of oral stories being passed on in fabrics or quilts?" I asked her. "It's my understanding that certain African fabrics have symbols in them that communicate a message and that when the Underground Railroad was in existence, slaves in America used a similar idea in making quilts."

"Quilts? What did they have to do with anything?" asked Nan, her curiosity apparent.

"Well, the slaves made quilts out of scraps of material in order to keep warm. Some people believe that the design of the quilt conveyed a certain message to escaping slaves. They would lay the quilt across a fence rail that would tell the slave when it was time to pack up, time to leave, or which way to run. The runaway slave could see it from a distance and know how to proceed. According to this point of view there were ten quilts in all, with different designs, that would guide the slave through. The slaves made them to help each other.[5]

"For instance, there's a pattern called Monkey Wrench. When a quilt with that pattern was hung over a rail, it meant it was time for the escaping slaves to gather all the tools together they would need for the journey. There's another pattern called the Bear's Paw. If a slave saw this quilt, it meant they should follow the bear's tracks through the mountains or woods to escape the slave hunters. The Drunkard's Path pattern meant to follow a zigzag path like a drunk. And of course, the quilts could be seen a long distance away."[6]

"Interesting. I have heard of our African cloth as sometimes having meaning," Sister Jane noted, rubbing her left temple, "but I hadn't heard that slaves carried this to America. It does make sense though. We've always used everyday things to communicate secrets, like what we call our 'talking drums,' and the rhythms of a blacksmith at work, or designs on fabrics used to make clothes. That's probably where the quilt idea came from. We have a kind of cloth called 'raffia' that has brown designs in it that represent a secret code."

"It's a fascinating tradition, Sister Jane," I said, excited to see the parallels in these struggles for liberation and dignity and in the creative response of people of African descent. And I was grateful to see that I could play a small part today.

Notes

1. Virginia Hamilton, *Many Thousand Gone: African Americans from Slavery to Freedom* (New York: Alfred A. Knopf, 1993), 68–70.

2. See Ann Hagedorn's biography of Reverend John Rankin, *Beyond the River: The Untold Story of the Heroes of the Underground Railroad*, New York, Simon and Schuster, 2004. Rankin is quoted in the front matter: "Thus have I been attacked at midnight with fire and weapons of death, and nothing but the good providence of God has preserved my property from flames and myself and family from violence and death. And why? Have I wronged any one? No, but I am an ABOLITIONIST. I do not recognize the slaveholder's right to the flesh and blood and souls of men and women. For this I must be proscribed, my property burnt, and my life put in jeopardy! Now I desire all men to know that I am not to be deterred from what I believe to be my duty by fire and sword."—Rev. John Rankin, Ripley, Ohio, 1841. See also *http://www.ripleyohio.net/htm/rankin.htm* for information on the Rankin House, which is now a National Historic Landmark and Underground Railroad Station in Ripley, Ohio.

3. The Reverend John Rankin is my great-great-great-great grandfather's brother's son. The lineage is as follows: Me (Elizabeth Rankin Geitz), my father (Oscar Lane Rankin), my grandfather (Oscar Tate Rankin), James Harvey Rankin, Samuel Rankin, John Rankin, to Thomas Rankin. Thomas Rankin's brother was Richard Rankin. Richard's son was the Reverend John Rankin who ran the Underground Railroad in Ripley, Ohio.

4. Jacqueline L. Tobin and Raymond G. Dobard, *Hidden in Plain View: A Secret Story of Quilts and the Underground Railroad* (New York: Anchor Books, 1999), 61–62. See also Wilbur Siebert, *The Underground Railroad: From Slavery to Freedom* (New York: Macmillan Company, 1898).

5. Giles R. Wright, a New Jersey-based historian, points to a lack of corroborating evidence. Quilt codes are not mentioned in the nineteenth-century slave narratives or 1930s oral testimonies of former slaves. Additionally, no original quilts remain. Giles believes Dobard has elevated folklore to historical fact. Dobard countered that the system would not have been written down as it might have fallen into the wrong hands and that a quilt was fragile and would not have survived over one hundred years. ("Did Quilts Hold Codes to the Underground Railroad?" National Geographic News, October 28, 2010, *news. nationalgeographic.com/news*)

6. *Hidden in Plain View*, 70.

CHAPTER 17

Nafi Ndika

I had spoken to several children, but not the young one with whom I shared the strongest bond. Nafi walked up to me dressed in a sweatshirt with blue and white striped sleeves, navy shorts, and scuffed-up black sandals. Putting my arm around him, I said, "Can I ask you some questions, Nafi?"

He nodded his head. I knew Nafi was shy, so I wasn't sure how our discussion would unfold, but I was determined to try.

"My name is Nafi Ndika," he suddenly began, proud and strong, "and I . . . I . . . I am nine years old."

"You're nine years old. Okay. Now, I was talking to Mobiya the other day and he told me about the very first night you came here to the Good Shepherd Home. Do you remember that?"

He nodded again.

"You were really little; you must have been about four years old."

"Yes."

"What was it like?"

Silence.

"You don't remember?" I asked, realizing that it was going to be more difficult to hear Nafi's story directly from him due to his age. He had come to the Home much younger than Mobiya, Carine, or Clemence and he was a good bit younger than them now, without their vocabulary or personal awareness. His story was no less important, however, so I persevered.

"Yes," he then replied, indicating I was correct, he didn't remember.

"What are your days like when school's in session? What do you do when you wake up?"

"I say my prayers, sweep the road, and then go to school," he said.

"Oh, it's your job to sweep the road. And what do you do when you get to school?"

"We do sports and learn things. Now I have a new school."

"What grade are you in now?"

"I'm in Class Six."

"Then what do you do when school's over?" I questioned further.

"I go to stay with my aunt for holidays. I help out with the family and the farm. I plant maize, corn."

"Ah, how do you plant maize?" I asked.

"You put two seeds in one hole," he answered patiently.

"And what do you dig with, your hands?"

"A stick."

"I bet that works well. So you spend August with them on the farm?"

"Yes."

"Nafi, Sister Jane told me the story about one time when you went home on holiday and made brooms. How'd you make them?"

"My uncle cut them for me with a knife and I cleaned off the stalks. I made 25 brooms."

"Wow, that's a lot. What'd you tie them together with?" I asked, gently coaxing words out of him.

"With bark from the branch of a tree. I cleaned the bark off the stick then tied the broom with that," Nafi explained, demonstrating with his hands.

"How'd you learn to do that?"

"My uncle taught me. I took them to the market to sell. I stayed there all day with my uncle who sold them."

"What kind of stalks did you use, Nafi? I still don't understand. Were they maize stalks?"

"It was this," he replied, pointing up to a palm tree. "I used my hands to clean them. You make a broom from the leaves that are on one big branch."

"Oh, I see how you did it now. And did you put a handle on the broom made out of one big branch?"

"Yes."

"A regular tree branch so it was pretty tall? How tall was the broom?"

"Like this," he answered, putting his little hand two feet off the ground.

"Okay, so somebody would bend over to use it."

"Yes, like this," he explained, bending over and making a sweeping motion with his hands.

"And what did you do with the money?" I asked, already aware of the answer from Sister Jane's glowing report.

"I gave it to Mama."

"She still talks about that you know, Nafi. What made you think of doing that?"

"Because she needed the money to buy our books."

"You know what Nafi? You're the only child who did that. Sister Jane is so pleased; she really thinks it's wonderful. Now," I said, changing the subject, "she also told me about your sister trying to take you away from the Home."

"I will go down to the bush and cut you a broom," he interjected, nodding his head. "I would like to make one for you."

"You want to show me now?" I asked. But he shook his head, deciding, as he said, "It's too far."

"Oh, okay. Well . . . are you comfortable telling me about your sister? Are you okay with that?" I asked once again, carefully.

"My sister wanted us to leave the Home because she didn't want to do any work. So in the night she tried to take me. Then my sister ran off all by herself to the village," he shared, ducking his head as if he were ashamed of what his sister had done.

"What made you say no?"

"We had no one, nobody to stay with."

"You were very smart not to go. Has she been back?"

"Yes, she came back so I told Mama."

"Are you glad you stayed?"

"Yes." He nodded his head.

"Will you come watch me play soccer?" he asked, reaching for my hand.

"Of course I will Nafi." And we walked down the packed dirt road he had swept that morning.

CHAPTER 18

Pregnant Pigs and Politics

Sister Jane came scurrying up the path one morning. "We just got more pigs," she exclaimed excitedly. "We've got ten of them and eventually they will be coming here. We're going to raise them up and use them for meat for the children. We will also sell some. The man who sold them to us, oh, he is a serious man. He knows how to take care of pigs. He got us ten and we shall be taking them eventually, because they must be pregnant before he sells them. That is his rule."

"Oh, so then you get two for one . . . or more."

"Yes, a pregnant pig will sometimes have seven, eight, even up to twelve."

"So when you get them, all the pigs will be pregnant?"

"No, there is one male—one male and nine pregnant. We'll be having thirty-two because we have twenty-two pigs now," she explained, wanting to be certain I had it just right.

Her morning's job complete, Sister Jane went inside the Home while Lillian, Nan, and I went shopping for supplies for the piggery with Randy. This was a day of great celebration—nine pregnant pigs on the way. Filled with joy, we piled into the Home's truck and were off for another journey back down the dirt road filled with deep crevices, which this time was slick with rain.

I was fearful we would never make it down the road safely as we veered from side to side. To our left, it appeared that dirt and rocks had fallen down from a hill onto the road and could do so again at any moment. To our right, there was no guard rail and a steep drop into oblivion.

I asked if the road was owned by the Home or the government, and was informed that it was a government road. Randy told us that

Sister Jane had been to the government offices many times to try to get the road repaired. No funds available, she was told repeatedly. This is the reality in a country with no infrastructure for basic road construction or repair. Still, this was a matter of life and death. What would it take to get someone's attention, a van full of orphans tumbling down the embankment?[1]

We arrived safely in town on our search for supplies, and I was delighted to come upon several people engaged in a political discussion, especially since my mind was already headed in that direction. Intensely curious, I loitered nearby while pretending to look at eggs for sale, piled high on a street cart with a white umbrella on top.

One man was clear that he liked President Paul Biya, while several of the others were in complete disagreement with him. "You are wrong, you are wrong," one shouted, dressed in a yellow T-shirt, baggy pants, and sandals. "Biya's a terrible man. I don't like him. He doesn't care for the poor. Right there in his presidency you see poor people around, but you never see Biya doing anything for them. Never! And you should see how they round up the street children when there's an official meeting at the government offices. They round them up and take them somewhere until the meeting's over, then they just let them out on the street again.

"And how many students are graduating every year? You are standing here," he noted, turning to the man next to him who was wearing a light colored suit and tie. "You're an accountant and has he ever given you any job? See the big mansions they are in? Those are the people with money; they take taxes."

A younger man chimed in. "All he does is take tax money. The government people are the only ones with any money. And corruption? I tell you, there is so much corruption all over Africa!"

"Let him get out. Let him get out!" the older man continued. "How many people are dying every week in Bakassi? Every week. It's our place and the Nigerians are trying to take it away from us because there's oil there. We've been living there for more than a hundred years. It is very terrible."

"Come on Elizabeth. We've got to go," called Nan, unaware of why I was lingering.

"No problem," I answered, sorry to miss the rest of the discussion, but not wanting to give myself away. Randy had found the supplies for the piggery and loaded them into the truck. We wound our way back through the crowded city.

"Have you noticed the signs?" Nan asked suddenly, as we rounded a corner. "Look at this red and yellow one up ahead. Randy, can you slow down? It says, 'Alpha and Omega Casino.'"

We laughed, knowing that in the Bible Jesus was called the Alpha and the Omega, the Beginning and the End. What that had to do with gambling we couldn't quite figure out—except that maybe it was the beginning of great fortune for some people and the end for others.

"And here's another one over there. See that blue and white sign? 'God's Own Hard Ware Center.'" Nan pointed to it out the window.

Clearly God figured into every part of the culture here, even commerce.

As we moved further away from town towards the orphanage, we all began to focus on getting back up the hill. I could hardly wait to share the political discussion I'd just heard with Sister Jane. Fortunately, we made it up the hill on the third try.

As soon as we got out of the truck in front of the convent, I ran up to Sister Jane, Divine, and Laurence who were standing outside with several of the younger children. To my right were several young girls drying soybeans, carefully spreading them out in the sun.

I related the conversation I'd overheard to Sister Jane verbatim; she responded with a look of wisdom on her face that was different from her earlier facial expressions. "Oh, but that's just a little of the story, Mama Lizzie. That's not the half of it, not just in our country but all over Africa. But let me tell you about Bill Clinton," she suddenly said brightly.

We looked confused. Why former U.S. president Bill Clinton?

"He's a great man," she continued, "a great man. We love him so much. When he was in power, the dollar was seven hundred francs here. The dollar is now four hundred and something, so we suffer a great effect. We depend on American dollars, so when America is doing well we are very happy. See the dormitory we're trying to finish over there for the children?" she asked, pointing to her left down the hill. "If it was in the time of Clinton it would be finished. Now we are not able to finish that building because the dollar is so weak."

"We don't know what has caused that dollar to be so weak," added Divine.

Suddenly it started raining, forcing us to move indoors, but the weather did not dampen the spirit of our lively discussion. "It is Bush," continued Sister Jane with anger. "It is Bush. He is the whole problem!"

"What about Hillary?" I asked. "If she'd won the nomination and were elected president, do you think she would have done what Bill did?"

"Who knows?" answered Divine. "She would say anything to get elected."

"I don't know," quipped Sister Jane, disagreeing. "She would have cared about the economy. I just know it."

I asked what they thought of Obama, who had just won the Democratic primary.

"Oh, Obama, he is our uncle," Sister Jane exclaimed with great enthusiasm. "We love him! We hope he is the next president of the United States."

"He's impressive," noted Divine.

"The whole African continent will celebrate when he wins," Sister Jane declared. "Oh yes, just you wait. And you know, many families here in Africa have someone living in America. His wife's in America, in Virginia," she said, pointing to Divine. "She's studying and working. When one family member goes, they struggle to get others to cross. They cannot live in peace anywhere else."

"What about Europe?" I wondered.

"There is too much discrimination in Europe," she informed us. "They don't give them jobs. They harass them."

Walking back to my room, I found myself reflecting on pregnant pigs and politics, the agenda of our morning as it had unexpectedly unfolded. The pigs signified the entrepreneurial spirit of the people of Cameroon, painfully juxtaposed against the seeming indifference and corruption that shrouded African politics.

As I rounded the corner, I could hear the children singing. They knew little about politics or infrastructure, but they knew more about faith and hope than any group of people I had ever met. The afternoon rain had stopped; sun was peeking through the clouds.

Maybe the pregnant pigs would win out.

Note

1. Poor roads in Africa were cited in the *New York Times* article "Homeward Bond" by Ngozi Okonjo-Iweala and Dilip Ratha (March 12, 2011) as contributing to the overall poverty of the continent. They write that 50 percent of the world's arable land is in Africa, providing Africans with the opportunity to feed themselves and much of the world, yet poor transportation infrastructure prevents them from getting their crops to market. The authors' proposed solution is for African countries to issue diaspora bonds to African migrants around the globe, which number almost twenty-three million people. With an aggregate annual savings of more than thirty billion dollars, these migrants could do much to help their homeland.

CHAPTER 19

I Am That Child

Gathered over bowls of hot soup and homemade bread slathered in butter, we settled in for more storytelling. "Sister Jane, will you tell us some more of your life story now? We can hardly wait to hear the rest," asked Lillian.

"More about me?" Sister Jane replied, raising her eyebrows and pointing to herself.

Suddenly reflective, she remained quiet for awhile. "Oh my dear ones, you make me cry." She put her head in her hands.

"We don't want to make you cry. That's not what we want to do," Lillian responded.

"I know, my dear, it's alright. It's just that it makes me cry when I think of the past and I see how far God has brought me. My story is just one among thousands of people throughout Africa. Many of them are still in the same suffering. Life is very hard for them and I am not able to help everyone," she lamented, shaking her head.

We assured her she didn't need to keep going if it was too painful. She insisted. "No, I want to tell you."

Taking a deep breath, she began. "As I said before I'm the oldest of eight children. I was named after my aunt Mankaa Monica. When she was thirteen years she was bitten by a snake and died. This aunt was my father's special sister because my grandfather offered her to my father, in a way. She was to be given out for marriage and with her bride price, my father would pay for his own wife. So it was very bad for my father when she died."

"Because he'd lost the money to pay for his wife's bride price," I stated, making sure I'd heard her correctly.

"Yes, because he was not having that money. As I told you my aunt Mami Mary found my mother for my father. He only came back home to marry her. They had never met each other before then. So they got married and soon I was born. They named me after my aunt who had died, so when I was born it was like my aunt coming back to life. I am told I have a mark on the right side of my stomach which she had on that very same spot. I am also told I behave just like her. So my father had the special love for me that he had for that sister.

"But this was for a short time. He became very disappointed with me when I couldn't make it up to his expectations. When I was growing up, a woman was only good for one thing—to give birth to many children. If a man marries and the wife is not able to give birth, he can send her away and remarry. If the man and the woman really love each other, the woman will ask the husband to look for another woman so that she can have his children for him. At other times the first wife will be the one to look for the second wife. But many times the man just goes ahead and marries as many wives as he wants. So the woman is only there to give birth; she's a production machine for children. That's it. That's her first duty in her husband's house and this was the situation my mother found herself in.

"I was born in October 1960. A few years later my brother was born. I was too young to take care of him, but I did. Then my sister Evodia came. By the time my sister Mercy was born, I had begun schooling, but I had to leave to take care of her. My mother would take me to the farm so that when she was farming, I could take care of the baby. When my sister Mercy was almost two years, my mother became pregnant again. I went back to school; then my sister Eveline was born and I had to leave school again to take care of her. It happened like this when all my sisters were born. So my time was half spent in taking care of the children and half spent going to school. Well, my father did not see this, for if he saw this he would not have all the time blamed me for not doing well in school, or beat me for not knowing how to spell 'Cameroon' at age ten."

She let that image sink in, and then continued. "I got my first pair of shoes when I was sixteen years, and they came from my own sweat. I gave that money to my father to buy me shoes. He went and decided to keep some of the money for himself. Instead he bought me shoes that I wore for only one week and they fell apart. As for dresses, I had only my school uniform, which I wore to the farms, to church, and to any other place I would go.

"After school if my father happened to be home I would go and stay somewhere waiting for him to leave before I came in, for fear he would tell me to bring my books then beat me for not doing well in this subject or that.

"I almost died when I was fifteen years," she told us, more softly, "but my grandmother saved my life. I had stomach problems, so I went to the hospital. I was told to bring 250 francs for treatment because I had worms. My father told me he had no money. My grandmother saw the terrible pain I was going through and gave me all her savings to save my life. This amount, two hundred fifty francs, is half an American dollar.

"My father would tell me he was ashamed of me, but I did not believe his words. I knew I could do better if he would only be a good father. I needed a father who could love me and I knew that that father could only be God. I decided I would give my whole life to following him. I knew a lot about God through my mother. She would tell us about the life of Jesus and how much he loves us, what he wants his followers to do.

"My mother would tell us what she suffered as an orphan and that it was only through the help of God that she survived. She would tell us many stories from the Bible. My mother had never been to school, so her knowledge of the Bible came from listening to her pastor on Sundays. With all of this, I knew that only God could be the solution to my problems," she explained, her entire countenance radiating a kind of joy and love most of us seldom see or experience.

"After completing Class Six, I followed my passion and began my search for this loving father. Despite the fact that I was not doing well in school, there was still the possibility for some man to marry me. This was the only reason my father would keep me. I was sixteen years, and being hard-working on the farms and other things would help me to have a husband. It was very certain that one would come.

"One day I heard my father discussing this with a man who had cows. The man was telling my father that he was interested in marrying me, and my father was telling him the type of cow he will be expecting from him. If this had worked out my father would have given me to this man in exchange for this big cow!

"I knew there were nuns in my village, the Emmanuel Sisters, who were Presbyterian. I had a friend interested in being a Sister there.

She was far older than me. I approached her and asked her to take me with her the next time she visited. She did and I was so pleased to meet with the Reverend Mother. She welcomed me for our first time with a very big hug. I had never had a hug before that. Never.

"The Reverend Mother and I sat and spoke together. I told her what I wanted to do and why I wanted to be a Sister. I loved the way the Sisters sang as they worked on the farms and other things. They prayed together. My older friend who took me there ended up getting married, so I finally went to the convent alone.

"When my father heard about it, he told me that it would never happen. I would never go to the convent. With many threats he forbade me to ever visit the Sisters again. In my heart I knew nothing would stop me from going there. Nothing! He asked me if I thought he got my mother for nothing. He told me that if I go to the convent, there will be nobody to pay him back for what he paid for my mother.

"So I thought of something that would make him happy. I went to him and said, 'Pa, do you know something?' He looked at me with a surprised look on his face, for I had never had the courage to stand up to him for something I really wanted. I told him that the Sisters had asked for him and really wanted to speak to him. That made him happy. I told him that they wanted to send me to do nursing and that after the nursing something very good would happen. This became his song.

"Whenever he got drunk, he would tell his friends how I was going to do nursing with the Sisters. He knew that after the nursing experience, my bride price would be higher. I didn't tell him the rest of my plans. After I had been in the convent for many years, he realized that I had duped him, since there was nothing happening about me doing nursing," she noted proudly.

"My mother knew that I was never going to come home again, and this made her very sad for I was a big help to her, taking care of the farms and the children," Sister Jane explained. "The day I left for the convent was a terrible day for her. She had just given birth to my sister Beatrice, but I knew I had to leave home. She was in tears. My mother's bitter tears have now become sweet tears. Today, my father calls me all the wonderful names. He calls me that Mankaa woman-man. He says only a man could do what I'm doing."

"I would say only a woman could do what you're doing, Sister Jane, only a woman strong enough to take risks who loved herself enough to do whatever it took to live a healthy life," I said, clear in my conviction.

She thanked me and looked down at her hands.

"Then, Sister Jane, why did you decide to leave the Presbyterian convent and come to America? It sounds like you had really found a home there," observed Lillian.

"Oh, my dear, you see it was like this," Sister Jane said, suddenly animated. "When I got into my thirties, I knew I had to help the street children, the orphans. They were all around when I left the convent. I saw them dying in the streets and raising their arms to me. I saw one little boy sleeping beside the road. I went over to him and asked what he was doing there. He told me that was his home. At that moment it hit me. Something inside me said, 'I am that child,' and I knew my life could never be the same again.

"I couldn't sleep at night for thinking about the poor children. I had to do something very serious for them. The Presbyterian convent did not have a mission to them and they were not going to, so I knew I had to begin my own community of Sisters to focus just on this work. To change things. But I didn't have the training for it, so I visited a monastery for advice. They told me I had to finish high school then go to America to study convent management. So, I went back to high school.

"So I went and studied so hard, I tell you! When they knew I was going to graduate, the monks wrote to a sister convent in Iowa. They invited me to stay with them to fulfill my dream of opening an orphanage and they sent me a plane ticket. They were lovely to me. I am still in touch with them. Anyway, I got on that plane and off I flew to America," she said, clapping her hands together with obvious delight.

"My dears, I had never even left my country—never," she told us. "I was afraid but I knew what I had to do for the children. Then I discovered the Community of St. John Baptist. After a short while with them, it became clear that this community was where I was meant to be. I was part of them; their care and love attracted me to the Episcopal Church. My home now. My home. I told you how things took off once I was with them and . . . here we are," she beamed, making a gesture with her palms up, arms outstretched.

"You know," she continued, still obviously excited, "I've written a prayer sort of like Clemence's, Mama Lizzie, but different. I would like for you to share it with your friends. Let me go get it for you." She walked into the darkness of her room to retrieve her treasure, and returned with this prayer:

SISTER JANE'S PRAYER

Lord, I wonder why most leaders are men.
I wonder why a woman is considered here as a good for nothing.
I wonder and wonder and wonder.

Lord, we have depended on prayers and faith, and you intend to answer them in a miraculous way. When I look at all these orphans, the ones this community can help and especially the thousands who are hanging around the neighborhood waiting for death to relieve them of their burden, I still feel very sad. I do not really know how to express my feelings. But all I know is that these innocent souls need to live like everyone else.

Lord, our earthly means can never be sufficient to rescue the lives of these orphans without your spiritual guidance. Open the minds of those who are able to bring world peace and who have the means to be aware of this situation. Give them the wisdom and the will to do so. Let them help discard the old-fashioned tradition that a woman is good only for the kitchen or as a production machine for children. Let them make it possible for these orphans to have the basic needs of life—shelter, food, health, and education. Let them know that every child, no matter where he or she comes from, regardless of their tribe, beliefs or colour, is equal to the other. Make the rich and extremely rich to see and feel poverty around them. Make it possible for such individuals to travel where there are such troubles and experience it for themselves and subsequently give a helping hand.

Lord, we pray that you should open the minds of our leaders and influential individuals to come to the rescue of the orphans and less privileged especially here in Bamenda, Cameroon, where there are over nine thousand orphans. Our community can only take care of fifty of them right now.[1] They should give them education. They should give them food. They should give them medicine. They should prevent them from dying or becoming public nuisances. They should give them free secondary boarding school.

Lord, I am tempted at times to ask you to make the rich to be poor and even become orphans for awhile, then to make them rich again so that they will be able to understand poverty, hardship, discrimination. But I always have faith that you have a reason.

Lord, I at times transgress by questioning why you make others have more than enough and others have nothing but death awaiting them. I wonder why our leaders do not take practical actions to eradicate this poverty. I wonder why a child is abandoned. I wonder why bombs are produced. I wonder why there is war. I wonder why there are terrorists. I wonder, I wonder, I wonder why you cannot stop all this now!

I know a lot of people wonder like me. Lord, I do stop wondering when I am inspired by the words *prayer* and *faith*. These are the two words that make us smile sometimes. I have faith when we always pray to you. I have faith that you will come and rescue this orphanage and the more than nine thousand orphans in this small region of Cameroon. I have faith that you will rescue the poverty that is damaging most Africans. I have faith that through our leaders, you will stop the wars in Iraq, Sudan, Palestine-Israel, Pakistan, and everywhere in the world where there is hunger and bloodshed. I have faith you will rescue America from the bad economic situation and give wisdom to its leaders to be able to promote world peace. I have faith that you will open their minds and give all leaders the means and will to act.

Lord, I am praying hard that you should make these great people to provide a secondary school for these poor orphans in Bamenda. I pray that you should inspire us and give us more wisdom, faith, and means to establish the annex of our orphanage in Batibo to care for children with HIV/AIDS, epilepsy, and other health hazards.

I pray that you should inspire all the poor, depressed, and less privileged to have faith and use prayer as their only weapon. I pray that you should provide more means and faith to the numerous people who have been giving us a helping hand to rescue souls. Lord, pour your blessings onto them. Let the change begin today. Let world peace begin today. Let there be real peace. Lord hear our prayers. Amen.[2]

Notes

1. As this book went to press, there were 130 orphans in the Good Shepherd Home and Good Shepherd Home Annex.

2. Sister Jane's Prayer was later published as "A Mother-Sister's Prayer" in Margaret Rose, Jenny Te Paa, et al., editors, *Lifting Women's Voices: Prayers to Change the World* (New York: Morehouse Publishing, 2009), 13–14. It has been edited for inclusion here.

CHAPTER 20

Spirit of Generosity

For three years I'd been waiting for the moment when I could say, "Come on Nafi! It's time for us to go shopping together!" One day I rounded the corner to the courtyard dressed in my beige cargo pants and loose-fitting dark brown top. There stood Nafi with his big, brown, expressive eyes gleaming, dressed in the outfit he had worn the day we arrived. He slipped his hand in mine, waiting until Randy was ready to take us on yet another sojourn into the city. Lillian, Nan, and I piled into the back seat of the truck, and we fit fine with Nafi on my lap.

Back down the slippery hill we bounced, with African music blaring from the radio, an upbeat song in one of the many dialects. Horns honking, thirty-year-old cars packed like sardines on the pot-holed streets, we slowly wove our way into an urban area five minutes from the Home. Suddenly, a crowded colorful bazaar loomed before us. Picture a state fair lined with one rickety booth after another stuffed with wares of all kinds. Imagine booths made of thin logs covered in bark, some with Nike and Adidas soccer clothes, others selling brightly colored African fabric of all hues and designs.

"Pretty fabrics for you. Pretty fabrics for you," men and women called from the stalls.

"I'll be back," I called over my shoulder as I followed Nafi into a booth that sold shoes.

Randy, the driver, mechanic, and now personal shopper, guided Nafi's selections. "You need some church shoes," he told him. Nafi nodded and smiled. "Here, put these on." Some leather dress loafers appeared—they looked very uncomfortable to me, but Randy was clear.

"Make sure he's got plenty of room to grow," Randy told the salesman. "It'll be a long time before he gets another pair like these."

"Do you like these?" I asked, eager to please. "Are they comfortable? Walk around in them a bit." After some lively negotiating by Randy, we bought them and moved on. I looked up to see Nafi already in the booth with the soccer clothes. Randy took us into a back "room," so designated by a homemade curtain of rough cream-colored fabric. The room was piled floor to ceiling with clothes, one bare light bulb hanging from a wire.

"Here Nafi, try this, this, and this," said Randy picking out numerous outfits from the tall piles. How he could see what he was selecting in the dim light I wasn't sure, but he seemed to have no trouble. I quickly left and wandered about in the front part of the booth. Soon I could hear Randy negotiating animatedly in the Bafut dialect with the owner. After about five minutes of haggling, they came to an agreement; I paid and we were off.

"Now he needs some church clothes," Randy insisted with a smile. The centrality of faith in the lives of these children was tangible at all times, whether they were saying prayers, singing songs, or shopping for clothes. In a country where the children have so little, they never seemed to forget the Giver of all gifts, especially life itself. We returned to the African fabric booth where I purchased vibrant purple and navy fabric with intricate designs for my son Mike's college dorm room. I wondered if the designs held any special meaning. Then we left the packed noisy bazaar and drove to a craft store that catered to tourists. Wood carvings of all shapes and sizes were abundant, as were purses made of straw. I found some wooden bottle openers shaped like turtles, fish, and pineapples—crude carvings with two short nails to open the bottle—and a beautiful heavy hand-made ceramic nativity set, painted in vibrant hues. Hand-woven straw trivets with African designs rounded out my gifts to take home and then I turned to Nafi.

"What would you like, Nafi? I'll get anything for you here you would like."

"A cross," he said softly and ducked his head.

"For your room or for around your neck?" As soon as the words were out of my mouth I remembered that he didn't have a room or even a bed of his own. He had no place to keep one personal artifact.

"For my neck." After some help from the sales woman, we found a small, ebony carved cross, very simple. "That one," he said.

"We'll take two."

The woman was thoughtful enough to find some leather string for us and we had our matching crosses—one for Nafi and one for me.

I then began the local tradition of bartering for all the goods I wanted to purchase. Back and forth the sales clerk and I went, until we finally agreed on a price for all my souvenirs. At that moment, Nan appeared around the corner, chagrined that she had paid the full amount. Randy had told her that bargaining was expected, but she wasn't sure how to go about it.

Just then Randy walked up laughing. "You should have bargained with them Auntie Nancy. They expect it. Look at all Elizabeth got; she knows how to do this. I might have to bring her with me the next time I go shopping," he pointed out, obviously impressed. I wasn't so proud. Why did I have to haggle in such an impoverished country? It wasn't as if I couldn't afford the full price—tradition or not.

On the way back to the Home, I wondered about the other children at the Home. We had brought a gift for each of them with us from America, but this was something altogether different. Would they be jealous of Nafi? Would he be embarrassed over his sudden largesse? I had asked Sister Jane about this before embarking on our shopping trip, and she had assured me that the children understood. "This is Nafi's special time. They will be happy for their brother. Some of them have special days also," she told me. And she was right. Nafi beamed from ear to ear when he stepped out of the van; the children gathered around him and seemed genuinely happy for him. Again, there was no sense of ownership or jealousy. They knew Nafi would share, and they shared in his joy.

I still marvel at this spirit of generosity among people who have so little. And I wonder about the comparative lack of generosity in America. Whatever has happened to us, it isn't good.

CHAPTER 21

Love and Electric Blankets

"**A toast to the pregnant pigs!**" I proclaimed, as we raised our wine glasses at dinner one night.

"Here, here. A toast to the pregnant pigs," everyone chimed in as we clicked our glasses together, the three of us with white wine from Spain and Sister Jane with her palm wine.

"What's it like for black people in America?" Sister Jane asked as our meal was beginning.

"Well . . . there can be an economic difference," Nan began, carefully choosing her words, "and there's still discrimination. The laws have changed, but in some cases attitudes have not."

"Even though there are a number of blacks who are professionals making significant contributions to our country," added Lillian.

"I can see that. Look at Obama," Sister Jane responded, nodding her head.

"There have definitely been many advances, but we're not there yet. You know, Sister Jane, there are a lot of layers to what you just asked," I reflected. "Nan and Lillian and I all grew up in the southern part of the United States where slavery existed only 150 years ago. I was born in 1953, which was only eighty-eight years after the Civil War ended."

"My dear, you're telling me all this stopped only eighty-eight years before you were born? That's hard to believe," exclaimed Sister Jane.

"It's hard for me to believe, too. My grandfather was fifty-two years old when he got married and his father fought in that war. We're not that many generations removed from it. Also, when you travel in the South today, there's still a lot of sentiment about the Civil War and negative comments about Yankees, or Northerners."

"Really?"

"Oh yes, it's still there. Also, there's an assumption that there's greater prejudice today in the South against black people than in the North, but that has not been my experience living in the Northeast for the last twenty-nine years. I've seen just as great, if not greater, racism there," I finished, with ready agreement from Lillian and Nan.

"Interesting," responded Sister Jane, nodding her head. "So Mama Lizzie, what was it like for you being born in the South eighty-eight years after the Civil War?"

"Well, it was complicated in some respects," I answered, and then hesitated. This was sensitive ground, difficult for many people to understand. But Sister Jane had been open with us about her history and now perhaps it was time for me to be open with her about mine. And so I began, unsure where my story would end up.

"Sister Jane, you see . . . I was cared for by an African American woman named Anner Weakley who worked in my childhood home in Tennessee. She spent hour after hour with me and listened to my problems. I loved her with a fierce kind of loyalty. She was the embodiment of unconditional love. Yes, she worked for my parents, but growing up I just knew that here was someone I trusted, someone I loved, someone who was there for me and never failed me."

"Well," Sister Jane began slowly, carefully, "it seems to me that you would have figured out at some point that she probably had no choice but to care for someone else's children like they were her own. It's not like she had a choice, did she?"

"Oh sure; I finally realized it when I started working in the inner city in the mid-eighties. I certainly knew long before then that African Americans were not treated equally, but it wasn't in front of me every day. When I started working there, it was a daily reality.

"I became conflicted and I felt guilty. Guilty for my lifestyle then and guilty for how I'd grown up and not seen what was right under my nose. I talked to my priest, who told me that my guilt was not going to help anyone, that if I was concerned I should keep working in Trenton and tell others what I was seeing. So that's when I first started writing about my experiences. Then one day it became crystal clear that I needed to do more. So I picked up the phone and called Anner. It had been several years since I'd talked to her and my hands were literally shaking when I dialed her number."

"So what did you say? How'd it go?" they all three asked me at once.

"Well I took a deep breath and said, 'Anner, I need to talk to you about something very important.' She said, 'Elizabeth, is this you? Is this my Sugar? Are you alright?'

"I said, 'Anner, I'm fine, I just need to share something with you. I'm working in the inner city now with African Americans on welfare, mainly women, and I'm there primarily because of my love for you, for what you did for me. Anner, you gave so much to my two brothers and me and I know that. You gave us your love, you gave us yourself, and I didn't realize.'

" 'Didn't realize what, Sugar?' she asked me, trying to figure out what I was talking about. 'How unfair it all was, Anner. It was an unjust system, left over in some ways from slavery. You didn't have a choice but to work in the home of a white family like ours cooking for us, cleaning our home, all of that. I just never realized how difficult it must have been for you. You spent more time with us than with your own children! Oh Anner, I'm sorry, I'm sorry,' I told her, as tears began trickling down my cheek.

" 'You're right. It was an unjust system,' was her quick reply. 'It was and you know what? You were a smart child. I knew that someday you would realize it. I didn't know if I would live long enough to see it, but I knew you would see it. Yes I did. You were a loving little girl. I saw it in you then and I like to think I put some of that love there. Do you know how proud Anner is of the work you're doing? I knew about it; oh yes, I knew. I don't talk to your mama much these days, but Emma told me, you know she's my cousin who works for your aunt Lillian. We know what our Elizabeth is doing and we are so proud of our girl.'

" 'But Anner,' I asked her, 'how can you feel that way about me?' 'I knew you didn't understand,' she told me. 'And now you do and I knew that, too. I knew this time would come. And I read. I read the paper and watch the news. That President Reagan is just hurting the homeless people more and more. He's cutting all the social service programs. It's awful. People are suffering and he's doing nothing about it. He doesn't do anything for anyone but himself and his own people.'

" 'Anner,' I told her filled with love, laughing between my tears. 'You're all over this aren't you? You knew all along what was going on,' I said, realizing how little I had known this stalwart woman who I had thought I knew so well. 'Of course I knew,' she responded with love in her voice, 'but it didn't change my love for you and your brothers. Not one bit, but now you keep on doing what you're doing. Someday old Anner's going to be dead, but don't stop what you're doing. You're doing it for me and my people. I know that, Sugar. See Anner knows a thing or two.'

" 'Well, there's no doubt about that, Anner,' I told her proudly. 'Do you have any idea how often I think of you? How much I love you?'

" 'I sure hope so and I thought so, but it certainly is good to hear it,' she responded.

" 'Anner, I'd like to do something for you, not just for the people where I work. What can I do for you?' I asked.

" 'Not one thing, except what you're doing now for the folks there. That's a gift to me . . . ' Then she changed her mind, 'I know,' she said. 'I'll tell you what I want, what I've wished I had for a long time: an electric blanket. It gets cold in here in the winter and I've always wanted one.'

" 'Oh, Anner, that's not enough!'

" 'But it's what I want; I would love that.'

"I thought about the simplicity of her request and was floored. 'Anner, I can't tell you what this conversation means to me. I thought it was one we could never have, but we've had it!' I exclaimed jubilantly, my heart jumping up and down inside my chest. 'Thank you Anner. I love you.'

" 'I love you too, Sugar,' she told me."

"And that's what happened." My food had gotten cold and my wine warm during the telling, but my heart was full.

"Whew," sighed Sister Jane, as she got out of her chair, hugged me and looked into my eyes and told me what words could not. It felt like a kind of absolution, one I would never have asked for, but absolution nonetheless.

Was it white guilt? After returning to America, I realized it was, but such guilt is a reality for many of us who grew up in the South during the days of segregation. People in our situation have to acknowledge the guilt, deal with it, then do something constructive with it, rather than deny its existence.

And while I also struggled with white guilt, I also felt love, deep love, in response to Anner's years of love and care for me. A love that transcended skin color, prejudice, and history.

After my sharing, we sat in silence for awhile. Then Sister Jane said gently, "My dear, I'm beginning to understand why you have so much love for the blacks. And you know what? If you had asked any old mother in my village what she needed, she would have told you a blanket."

"Really?" I responded, finding the connection curious.

Sister Jane moved on. "Where does Anner live now?"

"Oh, she's been dead many years. She died just a few years after I spoke with her."

"How long ago was that, Elizabeth?" Nan asked.

"Oh let's see, I made that call to her in the mid-eighties. It's been a long time, but . . . it took me a long time to get there."

"Well, it hits me that we have people working on different economic and social levels today," Lillian noted in her usual matter-of-fact manner. "We still have people who come to our house and clean. Many of us do and I don't see what's wrong with that."

"It's like the more things change, the more they stay the same," Nan added.

"We can feel sorry that they often worked in unpleasant situations, but at least they had a job. Let's be realistic," Lillian insisted, rather emphatically.

"Well, that's true," I responded, "but in some areas of the South they were often paid basically nothing back then. They were just given a newspaper, a magazine, or some ice to work all day. Or maybe fifty cents."

"Well, that wasn't true with my family."

"Mine either, but we need to realize that was too often the case. Even when blacks moved up North for better jobs, they were only paid a dollar an hour or so in the '60s."

"Well . . . okay, maybe you've got a point there," Lillian finally conceded.

"And I ended up dealing with a similar situation myself," I admitted. "When I decided to go to seminary, I had a twelve-month-old baby and needed someone to keep him while I was in class. Who applied for the job but an African American woman from South

Carolina named Annie? I had already had this conversation with Anner, so what was I going to do? Not hire Annie because she was black and it would look like I was perpetuating a stereotype?

"I spoke with a colleague who headed up the Anti-racism Commission in my diocese. I asked him if it would be racist for me to hire a black woman to care for my children. He said absolutely not as long as Annie was compensated fairly along with benefits, social security, paid vacation, and that sort of thing. In other words, as long as she was treated like anyone who worked for anyone else, then that put it on a different level than had been the case in my parents' day. And unlike Anner, Annie had a choice. She had worked at a day care center for sixteen years and had chosen this type of work because she loved children. She had gone to school to get a certificate in early childhood development."

"So what happened?" asked Sister Jane, brimming with curiosity.

"Well, twenty years later Annie still works for us and my family loves her a great deal, but the dynamic is different than when I was growing up. For example, I regularly talk with Annie about racism, how she feels about certain things, how she grew up. She told me about her brother being beaten by Trenton, New Jersey, cops and left for dead in the early seventies for no other reason than because he was black. She was pleased I had worked in the inner city, and she has encouraged my writing and helped give me a different perspective many times that's been invaluable to me. Whenever I write or preach about racial issues, I ask her to read it and advise me. She partners with me in my work on many different levels."

"You know, it sounds like that has a lot to do with why you're here, Elizabeth, but to be honest with you—if this is confession time—it really doesn't have any bearing on why I'm here," Lillian said. "My connection with Africa began more with a sense of adventure and a trip to Mozambique I took seven years ago. It's actually because of that trip that I was invited to go to Cameroon the first time, which as you know was four years ago now."

"I guess I thought we all had similar reasons for coming here just because we all grew up in the South," I mused. "Of course now that I think about it, that doesn't really make sense, does it? Nan, how about you? Why do you think you wanted to come here?"

"I've always wanted to save the world one child at a time. Where that came from I'm not really sure, but my daughter Preston just got back from working in a hospital in India. Her experience in a developing nation changed her life. I wanted to have a better sense of what that was all about, but I was afraid of traveling to a third-world country."

"You know," I said, "what matters is that we're all three here—learning from, working with, and helping care for these innocent children. What got us here is much less important than the fact that we're here."

"I really asked a tough question tonight didn't I?" Sister Jane said with a laugh, as she stood up and began clearing the dishes. Immediately we were all on our feet, carrying plates and glasses in with her, ready to help our sister in one task we could all share.

CHAPTER 22

I Will Die with This Child

We had talked about racism in America, but I also wondered about the hierarchies that operate in Cameroon. While she hasn't had to deal with racism at home, Sister Jane said the tribal oppositions could be vicious.

"There are different tribes, and many do not get along at all. Some think others are lower than animals. That's why here at Good Shepherd we accept children from all different tribes. As I mentioned the other day, our motto is 'May We All Be One.' That's not true throughout our country. We're trying to change that, beginning with the children."

"This mingling of the tribes here could have a lasting impact all over Africa," I chimed in. "Here they're growing up with love for all people. They're not learning what people in nearly every country in the world learn—that some people are better than others because of the color of their skin or their ethnicity or their tribe or clan. This could have an impact well beyond the Good Shepherd Home."

"That's my vision, Mama Lizzie. That's it! Even America doesn't have that."

"Right," I responded beginning to understand the genius behind the structure she had envisioned and established. "So, when you came to America, were you treated differently?"

"You know, I knew what I went to America for. Even if there was something like that I knew it would not be for long. I had to put up with it because this is what I wanted to have happen," Sister Jane said, her arms outstretched to embrace the Home around us.

"But you did notice it," I pointed out.

"I did notice it. Will you promise not to tell anyone when you get back to America what I'm about to share with you?" she then asked, softly.

"Of course," I replied. "These are all your stories to tell or not. Not ours."

At her request, I will not relate the stories Sister Jane shared with us. But unfortunately, whether you're a woman from Africa studying to be a nun, a hard-working middle-aged African American, or a black student living in the inner city, racial discrimination is still the reality in the United States.

Sister Jane was wise to bring up the issue of people of African descent in America. If we were concerned about her and the orphaned and abandoned children of Africa, shouldn't we be equally engaged with people of African descent in our own country? It's easy to keep poverty at arm's length, and even to romanticize it. "Don't do that to my people," Sister Jane seemed to be reminding us.

"What do you want Rodrique?" Sister Jane asked suddenly, turning to the four-year-old boy who had just wandered up to the dinner table. Since our arrival we had noticed that one of the orphans received different attention from the rest, clinging to Sister Jane's skirts, tattle-telling on the other children, and behaving as if he were spoiled. Uncharacteristically, Sister Jane seemed oblivious to his special treatment.

"Food. I want more food," he said forthrightly.

"Here, eat all you want; just go in the other room. We're talking."

Rodrique began to whine and clearly wasn't going anywhere. Sister Jane finally had to get up and take him into the other room herself. As she was getting him situated, Lillian, Nan, and I conversed among ourselves. We were concerned that such special treatment was not in Rodrique's best interest. The other children noticed it and obviously did not like it, to the point that it was impacting their relationship with him. On the other hand, we were very much outsiders and felt it wasn't our business to tell Sister Jane how to raise one of her children.

Before our conversation could come to a conclusion, Sister Jane returned. "Would you tell us about Rodrique?" I asked with as much diplomacy as I could muster.

"Oh," she said, her eyes brightening, "that child is much attached to me. He saved my life. You see, Rodrique was the first baby to come to the Good Shepherd Home, the very first. He was only nine days. I was giving him his bottle one night and suddenly I looked up and saw armed robbers standing in my room. I didn't even know they had gotten in; I never even heard a thing.

"'We've been sent here to kill you,' they threatened, 'but if you give us all your American dollars we will let you live.' So I held out Rodrique. I said, 'Look, we are here to take care of these orphaned children. That is all. Without us they would die. And I understand why you are here. It is not right that you have no money, no jobs. I do understand.' As I was talking I stood up on my bed and got some money I had hidden on a ledge high on the wall and gave it to them. Well, I think something touched them when they saw Rodrique and knew I understood how they felt, so they left. Plus, I had given them some money. Not nearly what they were looking for, but something. When they were gone, I was so frightened. I started running, running out into the night. Running everywhere!

"I could have left Rodrique and fled, but I resisted," she continued. "I decided, 'If I have to die, I will die with this child.'" The defiance in her eyes, mixed with the compassion in her voice, left me with no doubt that she meant every word.

Nan suggested that a security system would help on the property. "Oh my dear, I have one now," Sister Jane said. "We installed it after this happened, and the villagers will come running if they ever hear it. They will come running, I tell you." It was a relief to hear that a system was now in place, both for her safety and the safety of the children.

"Come on," she said, her latest story complete, "it's time for Evening Prayer with the Sisters."

The Sisters of Bethany is an Anglican Benedictine Order of nuns founded by Sister Jane for the purpose of establishing the orphanage. Each day they say Morning and Evening Prayer together in a small side chapel off the living room. Their singing was just beginning as we slipped in to join them. There on bare benches and on the floor were eight Sisters, including Sister Mankaa who cared for the youngest children. As we entered they stood up; African songs soon filled the air as they did simple dances accompanied by drum and shaker. Then Sister Jane began leading them in worship. This was holy space.

"Guide us waking, O Lord, and guard us sleeping; that awake we may watch with Christ, and asleep we may rest in peace," we said in unison as the prayers concluded.

"Rest in peace, dear Sisters," I thought, as we grabbed our torches and walked back to our guest quarters, escorted by the security guard.

CHAPTER 23

Vanessa Ipolla

"**Before I came here to the Home,** my mother was Sister Jane's friend," fifteen-year-old Vanessa told me, jumping right into our scheduled conversation one warm African morning. Wearing a hand-knit hat on a sultry day, Vanessa looked like the school girl she was, albeit a warm one. We were sitting on a ledge of concrete blocks outside my room beside the packed dirt road where the children play soccer.

"They used to live together when Mama Jane was in high school. I was still a baby at the time. After schooling there, Mama Jane went to America; that's where she heard of the death of my father. She later came back to visit us in our home, then went back to the United States again. While she was there my mother died, seven years after my father.

"When Mama Jane heard of my mother's death, she spoke to my two elder brothers. At that time I would come here for holidays and weekends, then go back to the village to stay with my grandmother. After some time, my grandmother could no longer care for me and she suggested I come here full time. That was two years ago.

"Life with grandmother was not easy. There was no money for food or school supplies. I used to fry ground nuts and sell them in class. This was so I could buy my school needs—books, school bag, and school shoes. My uncles paid my fee. I lived there for three years. When there was no food, we came to town to ask my uncle for food.

"My mother died in 2003 on December 24. I was gone that day and came home in the evening to do some work. As I was coming back, I heard people crying in the house. My mother was already dead.

"There were five children in my family. Before she died, my mother told my grandmother to take the two girls with her and let the three boys stay in our house. My eldest brother was twenty-one at the time. Three years later he was dead. On a Friday evening he went out and did not return. He was murdered by his friends because he used to keep the money he earned working. The others all put their money together and shared. When his friends found out he was keeping his money for himself, they killed him and took all his money. He was found in an unfinished building in a deep hole filled with water. His friends had beaten him, turned him upside down, and then put his head in the water. That was last year.

"It was so hard. I was so hurt," Vanessa continued. "My brother, my mother, my father—all gone. He was murdered in Yaoundé, and I never got to see him after he died. He was already decaying, so they just put him in a white plastic bag and zipped it up. He couldn't be put in a coffin because he was so swollen from the water in his body. I have pictures. Do you want to see them?"

"Of course," I replied feeling overwhelmed by what I was hearing. Vanessa went to her room and quickly came back with an envelope of very well-worn pictures. I wondered how many hundreds of times she had looked at them. "My cousins bought this plastic bag you see him in, because we had no money," she shared. "They put him in the back of a Toyota pickup to go bury him. And this is the house they removed him from. His friend found him. We suspect he's the one who did it but nothing happened to him. There was no money to follow the case, so it quickly ended."

Before I had time to respond, she continued. "Now here's a picture of my brother when he was alive, working in a restaurant in Yaoundé. We are of the Bafut tribe, so he looks Bafut you see. He was twenty-four when he died. His name was Alex Fidelis." Adeste Fideles: O Come All Ye Faithful. His name was Faithful.

"Now here's my mother in the coffin," she said. It was a simple wooden coffin with light blue lining. "As president of her church women's group, she got buried with a yellow cloth on her," she added proudly. "She died when she was forty."

Vanessa then showed me a picture of her mother as a beautiful young woman, holding her as a baby dressed up in a blue and white hand-crocheted sweater. I pursed my lips and held back tears as I thought of similar pictures of my mother holding me. I lost my mother to suicide when I was thirty-eight years old.

Despite the geographical, cultural, racial, and economic differences between us, I had felt something of Vanessa's pain, although I knew that my life circumstances served to buffer my grief. I was not physically hungry after my mother's death and no one in my family had ever been murdered. Even so, I had lost both my parents, one quite tragically.

As we sat together, Sister Jane's words began to echo through my being. "I am that child." Yes, I am that child, too, I realized. I am Vanessa and Mobiya and Clemence and Carine and Nafi and every child here.

As Christians, we believe that together we all make up the body of Christ on earth and that "if one member suffers, all suffer together with it" (1 Corinthians 12:26). I had never felt that oneness more acutely than I did at that moment. Here was flesh of my flesh, bone of my bone. When Vanessa hurt, I hurt. When she was abused, I was abused. None of us stand alone. We all stand together.

Vanessa showed me the last picture and explained, "And this is my father. He's the one with the keys in his hand sitting on the steps. He was the bursar at a secondary school."

Again, I was struck by how much these pictures looked like they could have been taken anywhere. I was equally struck by how different their fate would have been if they had lived in a developed nation. These worn, tear-stained pictures spoke volumes to me of the pain of those left behind in the African AIDS pandemic.

After a long silence, I asked about her life at the Good Shepherd Home.

"My life has changed. The Home provides what I need to go to school. I eat well. The people here are family because we all love each other. They're just like my brothers and sisters, and Mama's just like my mother.

"We have you, too. You help and encourage us, and when you come you show us the love. At least we know we have mothers who care for us. Our hearts are overflowing with love for you."

We sat in silence once again. Adeste Fideles. O Come All Ye Faithful.

CHAPTER 24

One Pearl
of Great Value

Nothing in my experience prepared me for worshipping with fifty singing, clapping orphans; eight nuns joining in with lively body movements and song; and one African Anglican priest in bright clergy dress.

I had been asked to serve as guest preacher for the Sunday service, and I was intimidated. What would I have to say about faith to people who lived and breathed it every day? This was one preaching engagement for which I felt totally unprepared.

In addition, several men, women, and children from the village were joining us just to see the "woman priest." Not only was I to preach, but I was to preside at Holy Communion, as well—something they had never experienced, as women cannot be ordained priests in Cameroon. It seemed I was not only bringing a message to the Sisters and orphans, but that I was representing all women priests everywhere to the gathered villagers.

Usually my sermons are written, although I deliver them in an informal style that belies the notes in front of me. Not this time; I decided a bare bones outline would be best. Thankfully, the previous afternoon I had tried to take a nap, when suddenly a complete outline of what I wanted to say popped into my head. I quickly jotted down my notes and knew the formal part of my preparation was complete.

Sunday morning dawned bright and sunny as I awakened to sounds of the laughter and splashing of fifty children taking baths in buckets and sinks in the concrete courtyard outside their living quarters and just below ours. It was clearly the most special day of the week for the Christian children, and they were dressed in the best clothes they could find that fit them. Some of the boys had on girls' dresses or blouses, but never mind, they fit. After a quick breakfast I was ushered down to the chapel to get ready.

Once we were in our robes and clergy stoles, we lined up outside the little chapel in the same courtyard where the children had taken their baths several hours before. We stood on the wet, sudsy concrete, while the beautifully dressed and clean children sat quietly in their pews.

With no prelude, Steve the choir director started playing the keyboard, the older boys started beating African drums, and the swaying, clapping, and sashaying of hips began as the nuns and older children in the choir, all dressed in red robes, sang, "Sell all you have, give your money to the poor, come follow me."

"We want to welcome today Auntie Lillian, Auntie Nancy, and Canon Elizabeth who are among us and who have come to share with us," Joseph began. "We are blessed this morning to have Elizabeth preside at Holy Communion. What joy it gives me to be here with a woman priest who can preside for us. She is the first to do so, you know. Yes, this is a happy day!

"Let us pray together: Almighty God, to whom all hearts are open, all desires known, and from whom no secrets are hid . . . ," and the service continued. There was a great deal more singing than I was used to, so when in doubt I just clapped and swayed as they sang, and hoped I said the right words at the right time.

The Bible readings were next. Eventually I stood to read the Gospel with two boys on either side of me holding white pillar candles. Before I could speak a word, the entire congregation suddenly started singing again for almost five minutes. I just stood there with the book in my hands, singing and swaying along with them.

When the last verse was sung, I lifted the book high and read the Gospel of Matthew, retelling the parable comparing the kingdom of heaven to yeast that a woman mixes with flour to leaven the bread, to a treasure hidden in a field, and to a merchant in search of fine pearls (Matthew 13:33–35, 44–52).

I then walked to the podium, looked out at the sea of expectant faces, and preached as I never had before. Sharing all I had learned from them, along with my prayers and love for them, my words had never flowed more easily. I ended with a message I hoped they would remember long after we were gone:

"You know," I said, "God is not an old white man with a beard. Aren't you glad to know that? Your Creator is not black or white or Asian or Indian or male or female. But there is one thing that God is, and that's love. Our Creator is love, and you all so remind me of the image of God as love. You emanate that—you are the embodiment of that love for one another. I bless you, I thank you, and I am in awe of who you are and what you do. Amen."

After a lot more singing and clapping, the service continued; I was honored to preside at Holy Communion. I could feel the witness of women who had gone before, the ones who made it possible for me to stand at the altar in Cameroon and to lead the ritual that would evoke the body of Christ in a tangible way. Gratitude flowed through me. As the villagers, children, babies, and Sisters participated, lifting our voices in unison to the One who loves us all, we prayed for one another, for family near and far, for the Home, and for Africa.

After more singing, it was time to receive the bread and wine. I could feel us become the living, breathing body of Christ together, a patchwork quilt of different colors and cultures. Yes, the body of Christ suffers together, but we also rejoice together. The holiness of that little chapel, with the worn pews and the sudsy concrete floor outside, surpasses every service I have ever attended. The One who made us all was made manifest in yet new ways.

The communion hymn refrain, "Oh God you are wonderful, you make it possible for us to the end," filled the air as each child came forward with hands outstretched and head bowed. Many raised their small heads as they received the bread and wine, their eyes telling a story of pain and joy, love lost and love found. "The body of Christ, the bread of heaven." "The blood of Christ, the cup of salvation," I repeated for each child, feeling the promise and transformative power of the familiar words.

Sister Jane welcomed us. Then Joseph spoke, describing our visit as a living testimony to the power of the One who created us all. "Their presence here is testimony of God's love for you," he said. "We have witnessed a very special event this morning. Yes, women have been raised up to serve as priests in our Church. Alleluia!" He then invited everyone to come for a final blessing. Each child, Sister, and villager came forward and the congregation sang, "There's a sweet, sweet Spirit in this place."

Finally, there was Nafi standing before me in his new clothes, with his cross around his neck and his head bowed, ready to receive his blessing. "Blessings to you, Nafi, in the name of the Source, the Word, and the Spirit. Amen. May you always remember that you are precious in God's sight, and may the peace of the Lord be with you today and always." I made the sign of the cross on his forehead and laid my hands on his head as we prayed together. Nafi felt fragile and vulnerable in my hands, and I prayed silently but fervently for God to strengthen and guide him for whatever life had in store for him. As I thought of all he had already endured and all he still might face, my heart overflowed with love for this child. My beloved child.

CHAPTER 25

Our Mantra

Following church, Steve, the choir director, came to find me. "Canon, I'd like to speak with you about something," he said, looking serious.

"Sure, come in," I replied, pointing to one of the empty chairs. Lillian and Nan immediately left. We had all been warned that Steve might ask us for money while we were there; they quickly figured out why he had come and decided it was best to leave.

I will not relate all of our conversation, but in fact, he did ask me and us for money, both that day and in numerous e-mails after we returned to America. A conversation of that nature was hardly the way I wanted to conclude such an uplifting, inspiring service, but it happened nonetheless. There's no use romanticizing the poor, or imbuing others with qualities that we ourselves do not possess. The reality is that some people living a subsistence existence will cajole, trick, make up stories, and do whatever it takes to get their needs met. Others will steal, as we witnessed through stories of the swapped van engine, cables stolen from the new dormitory, and wood taken from the bakery woodpile. But most people in need did not resort to such deeds.

During our visit, we heard many heart-wrenching stories of mothers dying in hospitals, children going without food, people sick and in need of healthcare. As difficult and painful as it was, Sister Jane had instructed us not to offer money directly, as it would cause an unceasing flow of people into the Home. Rather, we were to give any extra funds to her to dispense on a case-by-case basis. To help us comply with her wishes, we developed a mantra, one that Nan and Lillian and I would remind each other of time and again throughout our visit.

"We are here for the orphans. That is why we have come. All our money goes to them. No, I am sorry. I cannot give you money."

We *were* sorry. And yes, it did hurt. It's not an easy environment for a caring, loving person to inhabit. You have to learn to steel yourself in the face of the unrelenting pain, keeping focused on what little you might be able to accomplish if only you don't get off track.

It was not the way I wanted to end my Sunday morning. But it led me to develop a more realistic view of certain people and the range of responses to poverty, and gave me a more realistic view of my own limitations, as well.

PART IV

Lives Intertwined

"There is no tool for development more effective than the empowerment of women."

—*Kofi Annan*

"No love, no friendship can cross the path of our destiny without leaving some kind of mark on it forever."

—*Unknown*

CHAPTER 26

The Triple Threat

One sunny morning, we piled into the truck for yet one more adventure. Before we got to the bottom of the hill outside the Home, we had picked up enough people to fill the back of the truck bed. When villagers see a truck, they just wave it down and jump in. Soon we were chock-a-block with people, as Cameroonian music pumped from the radio with a rhythmic beat that matched our bouncing movement down the road.

As we rounded one bend, we heard the unmistakable sound of children singing and laughing. Then Sister Jane started laughing.

"What are they saying?" I asked.

"Oh, nothing, Mama Lizzie," Sister Jane quipped, as she continued to laugh and cover her mouth with her hand.

"Okay, it's something; what are they singing?" I was certain there was a joke on somebody somewhere.

"They're singing a song about white people having long noses," she replied and the rest of the truck burst into laughter. "It goes, 'White man, white man, with the long nose, hello, hello!' and that's the song they sing over and over whenever they see a white person."

"Why is that so funny, Sister Jane?" I was now laughing along with her.

"Well . . . because all the children sing that, even when I was growing up. You see, all the white people have long noses and then all the black people, you see our noses."

It had never occurred to me that my nose might look long to people in Africa. I suspect I was the not the only white person who considered my nose to be normative.

Still laughing with Sister Jane over the inside joke, and thankful for yet another "aha" moment, we drove through the city of Bamenda, where some passengers jumped out for stops along the way. Next we picked up Joseph and then Mary, a registered nurse. With everyone in place, we began the thirty-mile trek southwest to Batibo. On one of the many rural stretches of road, we passed several women carrying ten-foot logs on top of their heads. They walked with their backs straight, heads held high, no hands on the logs, grace in motion.

"How on earth can they do that?" Nan asked Sister Jane.

"Oh, my dear, they can carry more than that if they have to," Sister Jane, nodding her head wisely.

"I could never do that," Nan mused.

"My dear, you've never had to."

We drove on to Batibo to visit the Good Shepherd Home Annex. With funds Sister Mary Lynne received after her father died, they had recently purchased property for this new program. The Annex would respond specifically to the overwhelming needs of orphans with AIDS and epilepsy, providing a home and support services for thirty children.

Sister Jane said she simply could not turn her back on children with such need. "Somehow we will make it when the children come," she said. "We have to make this work." I could hear echoes of her childhood experience with the epileptic in her determined declaration.

Sister Mary Lynne had purchased the building to be used for the orphanage, along with a house next door for the family of the man who would run this very special home, Mr. Che Anselm Suh, a social worker and medical anthropologist. The orphanage consisted of one ramshackle, run-down pink concrete building with tin roof and brown stains on the sides. Bunk beds were in the process of being constructed inside. Mr. Suh's home was next to it, a simple concrete block structure with no furniture inside yet. There was a lone outhouse and an unusable kitchen in the process of being made workable. This place had a long way to go before children could be brought to live there. As soon as we arrived, I sat down to talk with Mr. Suh. Roosters crowed continually in the background.

"What actually brought us here were the works of Sister Jane," Che began. "She has a lot of pity for the poor innocent children, and my wife and I spoke with her. I told her I had been to a part of rural Cameroon where there are many, many orphans and suffering children with AIDS and epilepsy.

"There are a lot of cultural reasons why there are so many. First there's polygamy, which spreads the HIV around, so many of those children are left orphaned. Then with epilepsy there is a genetic relation to it. In a family of ten you might have six children epileptic."

"You know," I interjected, "I was talking to one of the children named Mobiya who mentioned that he was from a polygamous family. Now both of his parents are dead of AIDS, and his eight brothers and sisters are all left orphaned. Now you're telling me polygamy also increases the likelihood of epilepsy. I have trouble understanding why it's still legal here in Cameroon and a number of African countries. The obvious health issues are clear, and now with the AIDS crisis there are compelling reasons for outlawing it."

"Well, polygamy was started in Africa for many reasons, many of which don't exist anymore. But originally there were, it was then thought, sound reasons for the institution," Che explained helpfully.

"First of all it was very prestigious for a man to have many wives," he went on. "You had to be very wealthy to support a lot of wives, so it was a way of showing the world how much money you had. Also historically, it was very helpful in an agricultural country to have a lot of wives. They could work the fields, do the planting, weeding, and picking. As a result there was more food and more produce for cash crops, which in turn gave the man even more money. So it was a sort of cycle. One helped the other."

I recalled a connection from earlier in our trip. "When we were on our way north to the Good Shepherd Home from Douala on our first day here," I said, "we stopped by a palm farm that Sister Jane had rented and hired someone to run so she can get cheaper palm oil. She told us that the man running it just got a wife to help till the fields. It sounded almost like what we would call a marriage of convenience. I didn't hear anything about love or courtship, just that he needed help in the field so he got a wife."

"Yes, well, that's pretty much the way it is," Che offered. "People are trying to survive and they do what they have to do. Now that man you are describing would never be able to afford more than one wife, but he needed one to help him with the work. Also, let's be honest here. I don't want to embarrass you, but there's the whole sexual aspect to polygamy. For a man to have many wives, it tells the world he has great sexual prowess, and it also gives him a lot of variety."

"Right," I said. "I can see that, but I just don't see how the women deal with it."

"They don't very well. There's tremendous jealousy among the different wives; they fight over the man and they fight with each other. One of my childhood friends is from a polygamous family, and he used to come to my home and just cry. He told us of beatings he received from several of the wives who were not his mother and that it was almost impossible to be friends with his brothers and sisters from a different mother. The wives and children were all suspicious of one another. All his life the only thing he wanted was his father's love and attention and he never got it. Then he would have to see his father go off with someone who was not his mother.[1] It was hell for him really."

"I can see why," I responded, letting the day-to-day suffering endured by women and children in polygamous families sink in. Add to that the fact that AIDS and epilepsy are more prevalent in such families, along with diseases of all kinds.

"Isn't this outdated now in every way?" I asked.

"Oh sure it is. Many of us are now educated in Western ways, and we don't think this is right. Also, as our economy becomes less agricultural there is less advantage to it, but it's still legal. So polygamy has definitely increased the spread of the AIDS virus. In some places the practices used in witchcraft have also."

"I know some people believe witchcraft is used to give someone AIDS, but you and I know that isn't the case."

"Oh but it can be," he insisted. "About 40 percent of our population practices witchcraft or voodoo. Witch doctors sometimes insert medicines into people by opening their skin with a razor blade. The same blade can be used on many people. You can see what happens. Some families try to prevent this by bringing their own razor blade but then everyone in the family will use the same one and if one person has it, that's it. So witchcraft can also be a factor, just not the way some people think it is."

"And the belief that AIDS is caused by a spell of some sort on the person who has it causes the AIDS orphans to be ostracized and mistreated by their own families," I added.

"Right. The view is that if someone wants to see someone dead, they use witchcraft to send AIDS to kill them.[2] But getting back to polygamy; the fons of course flout their polygamous lifestyle which is a huge issue. They don't exactly discourage it. 'Fon' is our name for a chief. Wait 'til this afternoon. You'll see."

"I'm sure I'll learn more about this then, but how many fons are there?" It was almost time to leave and I needed information.

"Well, in the Northwest Province there are forty-six fondoms, but today there are only twenty-two sitting fons. One is the fon of Bafut, whom you'll be meeting this afternoon, and Batibo also has a fon. In fact, we just got a new one two years ago."

I decided to change the subject. "Now with epilepsy, is polygamy the primary cause or is more involved? There are of course people in Western countries with multiple sexual partners, and I haven't exactly heard of an outbreak of epilepsy recently."

"Oh yes, there's more. Here in Africa, tapeworm completes the cycle. When the tapeworm moves to the brain it causes epilepsy. They get the tapeworm from wild pigs that are not treated. You have to cook it very well before you eat it. But the people here have a culture where they love pigs, and they are not put in pens. Pigs are left to run loose, and most of the children do not have toilets. Their toilets are the pig sty. So when you come to the sty, you can see what the pig eats. Then when the pig is cooked, it is in no way properly prepared. So the people take back the tapeworm; it goes back into the person and up to the brain."³

"And tell her about when babies are born," added Sister Jane, who had just joined our conversation.

"Oh, yes," Che said, "most of the births are done at home and if there is trauma to the head, it can result in epilepsy."⁴

I couldn't imagine how he would decide which orphans to bring to the Home, with so much need. "Many of them are epileptic and also HIV positive and orphaned. We will take a child who is all three. Given the means we can have very careful screening, and we have to have that because so many people just want to give up responsibility for their children. Not every orphan is as needy as every other orphan, you see. Some are better off than others; they have relatives or other persons who wish to help them. So we have a serious screening process. We go into the home and ask a lot of questions. You can't believe what people tell you. You have to get behind what people are saying and find out the true story.

"When a woman is married to a polygamist, for example, a wife will mistreat the child of a former wife who has died, similar to what I told you about my friend. In fact, we have an instance of a child who fell into the fire; that little boy was not fed. And you should see this poor child. His foot is completely burned and one of his eyes is burned out. It is awful, really awful, and he's certainly not the only one in this condition.

"If a child's birth mother dies the other wives do not care for the child at all, and the father often loses interest, too," he concluded. "They will not get the child the drugs he or she needs, because they cost money. Not much, but they do cost something."

"But you will be able to get them for the children here," I clarified.

"Yes. Sister Jane is sacrificing to do that; we do have drugs available in our pharmacies. Some of the children are resistant to the drugs, depending on the level of epilepsy, but fortunately most are not. It costs five francs a tablet, which is quite reasonable, but so many of the families still cannot afford it. The problem is that the health center might be in the next village, and they have to walk two or three hours to get there, climbing mountains, hills, valleys. It's too far. They cannot do it."

"So I take it there are very few government health programs," I asked, though I had already heard the painful truth.

"It's really negligible. The government has neglected this. They have cut off communication; there are no telephones. They really abandon the children."

"But there are people like you and Sister Jane with cell phones. What would happen if you communicated this to your government?"

"I can tell you that the government response takes a lot of time. There's a lot of bureaucracy and you go on and on and on. There is also corruption, which is a huge problem in my country.[5] These people are rich," Che explained.

"I understand," I said with a nod. "To care for thirty children with epilepsy and AIDS is not going to be easy."

"No it isn't, but Mama Mary will be here too. There's no way I could do this without her. She has a real gift for working with children, and they love her. Plus she's a very dedicated, competent nurse. She knows exactly what needs to be done. So with the right person to work with, plus our faith to guide us, we'll get through. It will work. It has to. The stakes are too high."

"Okay, let's go," Sister Jane called. I looked up and Randy already had the truck running with Sister Jane in the front seat, Nan and Lillian in the back.

"Where to now?" I asked as I climbed in, filled from the day's activities already. My mind was reeling with all I'd just heard.

"To see the government officials here. They need to see that we have you."

Not completely understanding, I climbed into the truck as Che jumped into the truck bed, along with Joseph and Mama Mary. Soon we pulled up in front of a wooden terra cotta colored building with Cameroonian flags and the words "Sub Divisional Office Batibo" painted in yellow on the exterior. There we were greeted by a tall, thin man who looked at us a bit warily, but nonetheless ushered us into his office and asked us to sit down. Sister Jane proudly introduced us as her friends from America staying at the Good Shepherd Home, and she explained that she had brought us to see the new Annex Home for Special Needs Orphans in his community.

The official had a picture over his desk of President Biya. His demeanor told me pretty quickly that I wouldn't get very far bringing up the overwhelming needs of the many orphans in his country and the lack of government funding to deal with them. Instead, I decided to talk up the Home and the Annex we had just visited, in hopes of garnering support for Sister Jane's life-saving work.

After our meeting, we went outside for a picture-taking session with all the local officials. When we climbed back in the truck Sister Jane was jubilant. "They won't mess with us now. No way. They know we have you. They know we are someone now," she gushed, clapping her hands together and practically dancing in her seat.

I had not expected our mere presence to be that significant in her mind. I hoped her assessment was correct, as the truck turned north and we moved along the road to our next stop—Sister Jane's village of Bafut and a visit to the fon about whose polygamous lifestyle I had just heard so much.

Notes

1. For a compelling, fictional account of life inside a polygamous marriage, see Mariama Ba, *So Long a Letter*, Oxford: Heinemann International Literature and Textbooks, 1980. Ba writes from the perspective of the first wife, describing the hurt and anguish suffered by both the wife and her children when the husband takes a second wife and essentially abandons his children.

2. See "AIDS, Witchcraft and the Problem of Power in Post-Apartheid South Africa," by Adam Ashforth, 2001, at *http://www.sss.ias.edu/files/papers/paperten.pdf*.

3. Epileptic Research UK reports: "Scientists at the National Institute of Allergy and Infectious Diseases (NIAID), Maryland, USA, have now discovered that a well-known tapeworm causes epilepsy."

4. Brain injury resulting in inflammation of the brain is a common cause of epilepsy in all countries.

5. See *www.transparency.org/policy_research*. In 2010, Cameroon was ranked 146 out of 178 countries (with 178 being the country with the least transparency), and it was given a score of 2.2 out of 10.

CHAPTER 27

Toby Jugs
and Cowry Shells

It was market day in Bafut, Sister Jane's home village. "They have it every eight days. That way it's on a different day each time it's held," she told us, as our truck rumbled to a stop in front of a bustling market area.

Clearly this was the village gathering place and grapevine, a place to buy, trade, or barter what was needed to survive the next eight days. The market was packed with people buying, selling, and generally having fun.

"I used to sell things here when I was young," Sister Jane told us wistfully, looking around as we all climbed out of the truck. And sure enough, there were some very young children selling their homemade wares—little cakes, beaded necklaces, brooms like the ones Nafi made on holiday. Sister Jane was obviously proud of her village, her people. Everyone seemed to know and love her.

Lillian, Nan, and I wandered in and out of the rickety stalls jam-packed with goods, taking in the Bafut way of doing business. I expected to see people selling food of all kinds, but was less prepared to look up and see the local version of Victoria's Secret—a booth lined with hanging bras blazing in the sun for all to see. There were bras in every color imaginable and in all shapes and sizes, for women who were not ashamed of their largesse.

The next booth can only be described as the local drug store, with toothbrushes of all colors in their plastic containers hanging from a cord on one of the logs that held up the stall. American and European aspirin could be found, along with toothpaste, Vaseline, face creams, and locally made palm soap.

"Ah, Mama Lizzie," Sister Jane cooed, holding up a deep mustard colored square of soap. "This soap; it is so lovely. It will make your body feel soft all over, very soft." I knew Sister Jane could sell ice to an Eskimo, but I was a willing target. This was a great way to help the local economy while keeping my skin and the skin of my friends at home nice and soft. So I bought six large square cakes, the most I could fit into my already too-full suitcase.

Then I heard roosters crowing and children laughing. I could hardly wait to follow the commotion. As I rounded a corner, there were at least ten hens and roosters strutting around on the bare ground. People were haggling over the price of the birds. It was nothing like picking up my prepackaged chicken at the local grocery store.

But where was the laughter coming from? Eventually we spotted a man with a large, obviously homemade marionette that sported sunglasses and a bowtie. Wearing a floppy white hat, white tennis shoes, and dark clothes, the man could make the puppet dance, sing, and pick up coins tossed by onlookers. Of course we joined in, and the puppet tipped his hat to us as the operator offered us an ear-to-ear smile.

Around another corner I spied a huge pile of American clothes of all colors and sizes, some with designer labels. "That's a real problem for us," Sister Jane told me, shaking her head with a forlorn look on her face.

"A problem?"

"Yes, charities think they're helping by sending us these American clothes," she explained, "but it has really hurt our African fabric makers. People don't want to wear their native dress anymore. Now, I do, but most? No way. They want to look Western, Western, Western! And what happens? The people here can't sell their cloth."[1]

After about an hour it was time to go, as Sister Jane had shrewdly bartered her way up and down every aisle, buying special treats for the children that she could only find in Bafut. "Oh, if I come back without this cassava for them, they will not be happy with me," she laughed, her whole body shaking. With our cassava, many vegetables, and palm soap in tow (no chickens), we headed to the next stop on Sister Jane's tour—the fon's palace.

Who is a fon and why does he have a palace in Bafut? Like many African countries, Cameroon has both an elected and a traditional system of government. While Cameroon's elected president,

President Paul Biya, has been in office for thirty-five years, fons still govern throughout the country. The fon of Bafut is one such local ruler who serves under the jurisdiction of the government of Cameroon along with a secret society of approximately eight ranked male titleholders, providing checks and balances on the fon's power.

"You know, Mama Lizzie, our fon has thirty-eight wives,"[2] Sister Jane shared.

I couldn't imagine how he had time for all of them. "Well," she continued, "I am told that the fon has a calendar and he goes first to one wife, then to another. My cousin is one of his wives. And, some of the wives do not like each other. They all want their child to be the next fon, and so they are very mean to each other sometimes."

"That's what Che was just telling me. I had no idea your cousin was one of the fon's wives. I'd love to meet her."

"I will try my best."

After traveling for only about ten minutes, our truck rumbled to a stop. To our left was a large compound of pink concrete buildings with thatched roofs. Two very solemn-faced men appeared beside our truck wearing American clothes that were clearly worn. They quickly gave us an all-inclusive price for a tour of the museum, to be led by one of the thirty-eight queens, plus a native dance show and a personal audience with the fon. "It will be two thousand francs for all three," we were told, so we readily paid the fee. As I usually do, I then proceeded to take pictures.

"Stop!" one of the men yelled at me in a menacing voice. "The price I gave you does not include the privilege of taking pictures."

I was obviously taken aback. Sister Jane then immediately went over to the man and began speaking in hushed tones. She quickly came back to me and whispered urgently in my ear, "You'd better do as he says. They do not like you to disagree with them. My family still lives in this village and they could hurt them."

My eyes widened as I tried to absorb this new bit of information. "Of course," I said, extending my hand to the man. "I'll be glad to pay. I did not understand this custom of your country." If this was a custom it didn't seem to exist anywhere else I'd been, but he did not look friendly, and Sister Jane seemed genuinely worried.

Our way cleared, the queen made her way to us. The third queen, she was beautifully dressed in a long brown and white African dress with intricate designs and an accent of white braid. Hair piled high on her head, she was tall, slender, and regal. She appeared to be in her early forties. The tour began right where we were standing as, with great relish, she pointed out that the two tall 'Y'-shaped branches sticking out of the ground had been the scene of numerous executions and were somehow related to witchcraft.

"And that," she noted pointing to a thatched hut with a wooden cylinder in the center, "is our three-hundred-year-old communication drum called a Nighaa Ni Bifh. When the fon has a message for the people, still today it is sometimes communicated on this drum and everyone in the village hears it. It is called our talking drum."

It was strange to see this ancient communication system next to the cell phones I had seen nearly every person in Cameroon holding. Traditional Africa is still very much alive in the village life and governance of the people, as well as in their mindset.

Our tour continued inside the compound. The queen led us up steep, concrete stairs painted white; then we found ourselves inside the palace museum, a white two-story colonial building with green shutters, displaying artifacts that traced the history of the Bafut people from the 1300s. Wooden plaques depicting the genealogy of the fon's family adorned the walls, as did spears, fourteenth-century battle masks, ceremonial objects, primitive statues, and tunics covered with thousands of real bird feathers.

"And this," she announced, "was the throne room of my husband's father." Before us sat a horn chair, leopard rug, slippers, drinking horn, spears, and all the accoutrements of the head of the palace, all signs of wealth and prestige. She seemed proud of her husband's legacy—it did not seem to bother her that she was one of thirty-eight.

"And here," she continued as we walked around, "is a first edition copy of *A Zoo in My Luggage*, written by Gerald Durrell in the 1960s in this very museum when it served as the guest house for the fon's palace. It's a very famous book about his time here with Fon Achirimbi II, who invited him to lots of cocktail parties and dances. But that wasn't why he was here. He was here to collect animals from all over Cameroon; then he took them back to England and started his own zoo. He made us famous."[3]

We rounded another corner and found ourselves standing in front of a French antique curio cabinet filled with English Toby jugs, eighteenth-century pottery mugs in the shape of a man's head, usually one of the kings of England. They were used for drinking ale.[4] "And these," she noted solemnly, "were traded for our people." She stared at us, letting the reality sink in.

I felt the air knocked out of me. Still, I looked at the mugs, intensely ashamed. A Toby jug for a human life? How many times I had seen these same jugs in antique stores in the United States? At one time I even thought they would be fun to collect. No more.

From that disturbing place, the queen led us outside into the bright sunshine. As I followed her, squinting in the sunlight, each step felt like an effort, my feet like dead weights. Stopping at the top of the outside steps, she continued, "To your left and right are the huts where the queens and our children live. The fon has thirty-eight wives."

I wondered how she felt sharing that information. Was she truly proud, as she appeared to be of her husband's family, or was this an elaborate ritual for tourists in which she had no choice but to participate?

"And the building with the tall pyramid-shaped thatched roof at the end of the courtyard in front of us is called the Achum. It was built by the Bafut people when they first arrived from Tikari over four hundred years ago and houses the spirits of the fon's ancestors, as well as the bodies of three Bafut kings. It's the only building still standing from the original palace, which was burned to the ground by the Germans in the Bafut Wars. They helped us rebuild it from 1907 to 1910 after the peace treaty was signed. No one is allowed in that building except the fon," she concluded with a hint of mystery.

"Can we visit my cousin?" Sister Jane asked as we descended the steps. The queen seemed hesitant. Then she stopped, looked intently at Sister Jane, and answered, "Yes." As she led us into an area that was not part of the usual tour, Che turned to me and explained, "See that shell bracelet on the queen's arm? Every queen has one just like it. It's made of cowry shells, a regal shell that only queens and the fon can wear. When the fon likes a woman he sees, he has one of his men go up to her and put that bracelet on her arm. She then has to go with him."

I was incredulous. "What if she doesn't want to go or she's already married?"

"The fon's men make sure first that she is not already married, and once the bracelet is there, that's it. He's the fon," Che answered.

Soon we were inside a courtyard filled with thatched concrete huts. Up close they looked much different than they had from afar. They were dirty with hard-packed dirt floors, and the other queens were poorly dressed as were the many children. There was no grass outside the huts, just more packed dirt. The queens were hardly living better than the average villager we saw, nor were they dressed any better. None of the huts I looked in seemed to have furniture, and there were no doors or windows.

As if on cue, Sister Jane's cousin came out holding her baby, who wore a moss green sleeper suit with feet in it. I wondered how many of the fon's other children had worn the same outfit. Sister Jane's cousin was wearing a navy and white striped jumper with buttons up the front, several missing, and blue sandals. Hair loosely piled on her head, she wore the cowry shell bracelet prominently displayed on her left wrist. The two cousins seemed glad to see one another and chatted about old times, family, and friends. As I shook this woman's hand in greeting, I could only wonder if she was lonely here, away from all her family, living with thirty-seven other wives and over a hundred children.

The third queen who served as our tour guide was always at our elbow. "Time to go now for the show!" she soon called, as she led us into an inner courtyard where we would soon see a dance show and meet the fon. We sat on concrete benches attached to the courtyard walls with a space for the show to take place in the center.

Outside the courtyard waiting to perform were about a dozen of the fon's many children dressed in soccer clothes and sneakers. An African drum beat echoed off the courtyard walls. The children played a forerunner of the xylophone made of thick boards of different lengths, laid out on long sticks on the ground.

A group of older teens appeared wearing traditional African dress over their soccer clothes. Their feathered tunics looked like the ones we'd just seen, and they wore large wooden masks on their heads—an elephant head to symbolize wealth, a gigantic face, an alligator head. Two young men were on stilts, jumping high on one leg in time to the drumming. Sister Jane and the Cameroonians with us were clapping and laughing in time to the drumbeat, and we were soon caught up in the percussion and the moment. Without warning, Che started dancing with them after dropping some money in a cap that had been placed on the ground.

"Go, Mama Lizzie, go!" a laughing Sister Jane called to me.

Then Randy went up, as did Sister Jane. Soon I was on my feet with Lillian and Nan, dropping coins and bills in the hat and swaying with the drumbeat. We loved it and they loved our obvious enjoyment even more. Soon we were all in a conga line dancing, clapping and moving around the circle as stilt men hovered and bounced over our heads. Something ancient and rhythmic began to flow through us, and now the previously sullen third queen called out as she pointed at me, "You, you're one of us! You're African! You dance like us!" Continuing to dance, I felt at one with my sisters and brothers . . . in spite of the Toby jugs a few hundred yards away. In spite of the thirty-eight queens with the cowry shell bracelets that announced the Fon's claim on them. In spite of it all.

The drumming stopped; we hugged and sat down. Out came a large, very important-looking wicker chair with a fan back, unquestionably for the fon and for our audience with him. The drumming began again—but no fon. The drumming continued—no fon. Some of the dancers went back into one of the huts and came back. Still—no fon. He never did appear. Whatever the reason, I did not care. My heart was still beating in time to a drumbeat that had sounded throughout the centuries—a drumbeat that called people together, warned them of danger, and shared good news. On and on it went within me as we said our goodbyes, climbed back into the truck, and headed home to see the children once again.

As we continued to bounce along down the road, in spite of the celebratory mood, I could not forget the Toby jugs traded for slaves or the cowry shell bracelets that had been placed on the future queens' wrists, surely without their consent at times.

"Sister Jane, does your cousin ever talk to you about life inside the fon's palace?" I asked, intensely curious.

"Sometimes she does, but not often. The fon is thirty years older than she is or even more. She thinks he treats her better than if she were married to an ordinary man, but even so things are in some ways very difficult for her, and she just has to accept the way things are. If she leaves the palace, her family will be in trouble with the fon, and so she just has to make herself happy. I have never heard of any of the wives being allowed to leave. There is always a lot of jealousy among them, too, but in spite of that they're all pretty much stuck there."

"And of course it's not just the fon who has a lot of wives," contributed Lillian. "I visited Cameroon as a tourist about fifteen years ago, and we took a tour through a compound of a man who had forty wives. He wasn't royalty, just wealthy. I asked our guide how he kept all the wives straight, and she told me he had a calendar to be clear which wife he would be with on which night, just like Sister Jane said the fon does."

As we made our way back to the Good Shepherd Home on the rough, winding, paved, pot-holed roads, it occurred to me that it was no surprise that people here had problems with Sister Jane's authority as a woman.

At dinner that evening, my reflections found voice. "You know, Sister Jane, this day was filled with so many contrasting images. Two threads seem to stick out in my mind though: witchcraft and polygamy.

"The belief in and use of witchcraft by some Africans plays a larger role than I previously thought. First it's used to impede progress, like the man who tried to scare you and the sisters away by using it, and the other man who tried to poison you. Then our orphans here are doubly ostracized because some people believe their parents contracted AIDS by having a spell cast on them. Add to that what Che told me today, that some practices used in witchcraft—like the use of dirty razor blades—actually can spread the AIDS virus, and it's a vicious cycle."

"Oh very vicious, I tell you," Sister Jane agreed. "Witchcraft is illegal here, but that doesn't stop it and even people who would never practice it, like our Sisters, are afraid of it. It is still part of our culture, with about 40 percent of our population believing in it. We're trying to do our part to let people know that there is another way, through God, but that's not our primary purpose here. Our purpose is to save the children's lives. If people see what we have and want to learn more about us, that's fine, but we do not proselytize. That just gets too complicated. All our energies are directed to saving the orphans, one child at a time."

As usual, her approach seemed both realistic and sensible to me. I continued, "Che was also clear that polygamy has greatly contributed to the AIDS pandemic, as well as to the prevalence of epilepsy. Both seem to create orphans who end up on the streets, in your Home, or worse—dying. Is anything being done to change this outdated institution? It seems to me that the fon, as a leader, is glorifying the very institution that's ravaging his country."

"No, nothing's being done; it's always been this way. It is considered part of our culture and the fon has a lot of power. If the wives were to try to leave, it would be very bad for them and for their families," she commented.

"What about women in polygamous marriages to ordinary citizens like Lillian mentioned, people who are not the fon? I guess I can't understand why they would do this in the first place."

"If you live in the bush and you're hungry, you do a lot of things to survive. Also a lot of times the first wife gets married and does not know her husband plans to take more wives. She then has a choice. She can either stay and put up with the other wives, or she can divorce the man. Most do not divorce; no, they do not divorce," she said, shaking her head in sadness.

Notes

1. See Dambisa Moyo, *Dead Aid: Why Aid Is Not Working and How There Is a Better Way for Africa*. She suggests that foreign donors buy from local producers rather than send goods to developing nations, which can put some local businesses out of business. If the manufacturing capabilities are not available locally, or not large enough to meet the demand, perhaps the solution is to "buy locally first, then supplement."

2. See Rebecca Hourwich Reyher, *The Fon and His Hundred Wives*, Garden City, New York: Doubleday, 1952. The full text of this fascinating memoir can be downloaded for free at *www.archive.org/details/fonandhishundred002372mbp*. Reyher's journey to Bamenda to discover the true effects of the fon of Bikom's polygamous establishment on the rights of his wives and African women in general was generated by widely reported news accounts of an English nun, Sister Loretta, in a story called "Just Cargo."

3. Durrell collected exotic birds, chimpanzees, apes, rare lemurs, antelopes, pygmy mongoose, pythons, and toads on his 1948 Cameroonian excursion recorded in *A Zoo in my Luggage*. He did not collect the larger game that can still be viewed in parts of Cameroon today. For information on a safari to this area of the country, see page 173.

4. Toby jugs originated in the eighteenth century and are a pottery jug in the form of a seated person, or the head of a recognizable person, often an English king. Typically the seated figure is a heavyset white man with gray hair in eighteenth-century attire, holding a mug of beer in one hand and a pipe in the other.

CHAPTER 28

Cyrille Kwetche

The sky had split wide open and it was raining hard when I spoke with sixteen-year-old Cyrille Kwetche. Every nook and cranny indoors was filled with children, but we found a vacant spot on the lower level of the unfinished dormitory, with its cinder block walls and rubble strewn across the dirt floor. Wearing a red basketball shirt, black gym shorts, and sneakers, Cyrille brought two chairs inside for us and helped me carefully climb down into the bottom level through an unfinished window. I was immediately struck by how cool it was. As soon as we sat, he began.

"I grew up here in Bamenda with my mother and father. When I was seven, my father died. I didn't get to see him when he died. He was too far away in a hospital and we couldn't get to him. They took him to a village in the Southwest Province of Cameroon. Later I saw where they buried him. I was then living with my mother, two brothers, and one sister in Bamenda," he shared in a matter-of-fact, this-is-just-the-way-it-is tone.

"After Dad died, nine months later my mother became seriously ill. She was ill for four months, and then she died. She died in the village because there was not enough money to take her to a hospital. She wasn't able to do odd jobs to get enough money to get into the hospital. When she got sick, we went to stay with my grandmother in the Southwest Province. We are from the Mouck tribe there.

"My grandma was my father's mother. My mother's mother didn't like us. She didn't care about us. When my mother was sick, she never came to see us. My father's mother fed us and paid our school fees. One year after Father died, Mother died. I was six.

"My father was a teacher but later retired and was a truck driver. My mother was a hairdresser. They were so nice to us; we were a happy family. When my father died, I felt I'd lost all I had, but my mother gave us confidence.

"I was there the day my mother died; it was four o'clock in the afternoon. I saw her die. She didn't say anything to us. Grandma was feeding her, giving her a bath; all we could do was help Grandma on the farm and fetch wood and water.

"When my mother died, I didn't know what to do. I thought I was going to die also. All of us were sad because we lost our mother. My little brother and sister were too small to understand, but I understood. I knew both my parents were gone from this earth forever."

Looking more like twenty than sixteen, with bulging muscles and heavy stubble on his round face, he continued, "We then went to stay with my uncle, my father's brother. Other relatives came to take us, but Grandma refused because they wouldn't treat us well. Our uncle we stayed with clearly did not like us. He maltreated us and wouldn't pay our school fees. He treated us like slaves and expected us to do all the work. We had to spray his farm to kill the insects and work in the fields all day, every day; we never got to take a break regardless of how tired or hungry we were.

"When I was ten, I helped my grandfather do odd jobs to get money; my pay for a full day was three dollars. But I kept working to have something to live on. There was one big compound with several houses in it where my grandfather lived, so we went back to live with him for four years.

"My aunt was living here in Bamenda. She came to the Southwest Province and asked to take my picture, but she didn't tell me why. After some months, she told me I was coming with her. When we arrived, we came here to the Good Shepherd Home, which was a total surprise to me.

"Auntie Lillian was visiting. They gave me some food and took me down to meet the other children. There were only eight of them plus me. I was twelve years old. I was very happy to see the children. They showed me love. We then lived together for three days. If I liked the place, I was told I could go and prepare to come back. As I was about to leave, Sister Jane gave me money for dresses and shoes because I didn't have any. I was very happy; I told my grandmother I really wanted to come here. I stayed in the village one week then got to come back to Good Shepherd Home."

Cyrille beamed as he offered the more recent details. He was visibly relaxing and seemed to be enjoying our discussion now.

"Mother Jane loves us," he continued, brightly. "I was very happy to be here. Fortunately, my uncle in the village couldn't say anything because my grandmother had made the decision. He didn't want me to come here. He was afraid I would never see his family again, but all of the children here go home for a month during the holidays when school's out so he had nothing to worry about.

"I was the first son here to go to secondary school. I was doing well in school and Mother Jane was proud of me. I just took a difficult examination last month. Seven hundred sixty-five kids took it; only forty-five passed and I was one of them. The exam is to promote you to go higher so I'm now going to high school in September," he told me, filled with pride, sitting taller now, back erect, feet firmly planted on the floor.

"I want to be an engineer; I love the profession. I want to help people, too; like the junior children here who are still growing. I also play basketball in school and love the game. I started it in Form Three and played on our school team. I aspire to have a scholarship in basketball someday. I'm 1.8 meters tall, approximately 5'11".

"I have morning duties here like all the children. I feed the rabbits, along with Mobiya, clean the road and house, then take a bath. After school we eat lunch here, because lunch is not served in the schools. Then we take a nap. In the evening we study in our rooms. When the lights go out, we use candles to study some more. The little ones go to bed at 9:00 p.m.; the big ones continue reading books. We go to sleep around 10:30 or 11:00 p.m., then get up at 5:00 a.m."

Brimming with pride, I assured him his growth into such a responsible, kind, and generous young man had impressed me and everyone at the Home.

"Yes," he replied, ducking his head. "I know I've changed. I know . . . in a lot of ways."

Then he grabbed the two chairs and helped me carefully climb back out through the window.

CHAPTER 29

Infrastructure Breakdown

Breakfast was always a treat for Sister Jane's guests. In addition to her many other talents, she was a mean pancake maker. As usual, the food was surpassed only by the lively conversation.

"Okay, everyone," Sister Jane suddenly proclaimed, clapping her hands together. "Today I want Randy to take you to see our closest hospital. There's an AIDS ward there, a family planning clinic, and a morgue."

After a fifteen-minute drive, we found ourselves on a curved road leading to the hospital grounds. Once inside the gates, I was struck by the beauty and grandeur of the poinsettia trees and lantana bushes lining the road. In contrast to the small Christmas poinsettias we have in the United States, these trees were at least seven feet tall, while the lantana bushes were about five feet tall and extremely full. Cameroon is a lush, tropical country after all, which is easy to forget in the midst of daily life there.

We came to a stop in front of the hospital, climbed out of the truck, and Randy took us to an office area. About thirty people were lined up outside, sitting on plain wooden benches. Out came a short man with a moustache and short hair, dressed in a white lab coat. I initially mistook him for a doctor, but he was actually a nurse. "I'm Alain," he said, as he began the tour.

The facility he showed us was large and clean but very sparse and obviously lacking in medical supplies and basics like regular beds. Separate male and female wards were designated by large green and yellow hand-painted signs. Inside we found patients housed in large rooms containing twenty double partitions with an aisle in the center of the room. There were four beds on each side of the partition— metal cots with ¾-inch thick mattresses and thin, rusty coil springs.

We were told that patients got no food in the hospital unless a friend or relative brought it to them. Hospital gowns? There didn't seem to be such a thing. Rather people were lying atop the thin mattresses in their clothes, some with intravenous fluids going in their arms, others bandaged, still others talking to visitors.

The nurses were all men in white lab coats, obviously very proud of their profession. "We have a new private-bed wing for those who can afford it, along with a family planning center and an AIDS clinic," Alain informed us. "There are fifty thousand orphans in the Northwest Province of Cameroon, mostly from AIDS," he shared as our tour continued. "Three NGOs [non-governmental organizations] surveyed the area and they came up with this figure."

Since he didn't have clearance to take us to view the rest of the facility, Alain took us back to his office for deeper discussion. Hanging outside his door was a large sign in a combination of red, black, and aqua-blue letters written partially in Pidgin English:

AIDS NO BE PUNISHMENT!!!
NA SICK
Millions of HIV/AIDS Victims are:
Faithful Husbands and Wives
Innocent Little Children
Diligent Health Workers
Religious Men and Women of Integrity
THESE PEOPLE ARE NOT NECESSARILY IMMORAL
HIV/AIDS IS NOT A MORAL DISEASE!!!

"Tell me about this sign," I said.

"Well, people here you see . . . AIDS is a big stigma. People do not talk about it if they have it, if someone in their family has it, or if someone in their family has died of it. People will think badly about the whole family and, of course, there is still the belief in some parts that it is the work of witchcraft.

"You see what we are saying here on the sign is that it is not a punishment; the persons who have it are just like everyone else. There should be no stigma attached. Until the stigma is gone and people understand what they need to do to prevent it, then we will continue to have a huge death toll from it."

"Is your government involved in AIDS prevention and education?" Nan asked.

"Yes, we have to be. Cameroon has the second highest incidence of AIDS in West Africa. In 2001," Alain explained, "the government of Cameroon signed the 'Declaration of Commitment' to set targets and goals to fight AIDS in partnership with all sectors of society, including the United Nations. We now have a five-year strategic plan that operates at all levels, from grassroots up through the provincial level. We also have mobile screening units."

"How many people in Cameroon are infected with HIV/AIDS?" I asked.

"Over half a million—540,000 to be exact."

"Now, what percentage of the population is that? It's not as high as in some African countries, is it?" asked Lillian.

"No, but it's pretty high here in the Northwest Province. In the country overall, we are aware of 5.5 percent of the population being infected. Here that percentage jumps to 8.7 percent and it's worse among women. In our province, almost 12 percent of the total population of women have AIDS, while only about 5 percent of the men are infected."

"I would have thought it was the opposite," I noted. "Why is this?"

"Let me show you a booklet put out by our ministry of public health," he said, pulling out a lime-green booklet with graphs, maps, and words of warning in pink, aqua, and pale green bubbles. "The booklet states that 'the Fons, Religious, and Opinion Leaders' can make behavior change happen by 'advocating and ensuring change in socio-cultural factors that enhance the propagation of HIV such as' and there's a long list. Now, look at these factors that affect women: early and forceful marriages, polygamy, lack of decision-making power by the women, widow cleansing,[1] neglect and abandonment of wives, tolerating male promiscuity, condoning actions of rape, the strong desire to have a male child, and early teenage pregnancies.

"The culture of male sexual dominance here is a big issue in the spread of AIDS," he acknowledged. "Women have little say over whether their partners use protection. Their wishes are not respected. As long as that level of male dominance continues, the rapid spread of the disease will continue."

"And this is certainly not the only country where that's a factor," Nan offered.

"Oh no, it's definitely not. A recent study in Africa has shown us that forced sexual activity with drunken husbands was most often cited by women as times when they felt they had been exposed to the virus, as many reported believing that their husbands had more than one sexual partner, either through polygamy or infidelity. Male aggression and a desire to dominate women is unfortunately the norm," he said.[2]

"Isn't it ironic that the fons are being asked to help change this culture when they have polygamous marriages themselves, force young women into marriage by putting a cowry shell bracelet on them, and give the women no decision-making powers?" I asked. "They're breaking every one of the rules they're being asked to help change."

"Yes, so you see; it will be up to the religious and opinion leaders."

"How about the government leaders?"

"At least they've put out this brochure, which is a first step, but it's hardly enough," he said. "We need people to advocate for these things publicly, not just the health organizations."

"That's for sure," I replied, feeling anger welling up within me on my sisters' behalf. I decided to discuss this further with Sister Jane.

After the tour ended, we thanked Alain for his time and patience. We then walked back to our truck and saw a car piled at least six feet high on top and just as high in the trunk with suitcases, vegetables, and all manner of things spilling out everywhere. The family was picking up a very young woman holding what appeared to be a newborn baby carefully wrapped in a blue blanket.

Unlike a gathering of relatives excited about the new life they were bringing home, each face was solemn, etched with sorrow. There was no wiggling, no sound coming from the little bundle. The woman who had just given birth was bent over as if she carried the weight of the world on her tiny shoulders. I wondered if she'd been denied a medical kit for delivery in the manner Sister Jane had related to us. I wondered if she'd had any prenatal care. Her cheeks were sunken and she seemed to be moving in a fog, clutching her baby tightly.

As we headed back down the drive, the poinsettia trees outside did not look as bright, the lantana bushes as full. Their beauty could not mask the poor medical care inside the facility. For awhile we just sat in silence as our truck wound its way through the busy streets of Bamenda.

"What do you think might have happened there, Randy? Do you think that baby was dead?" asked Nan.

"Yes, I would say so. You know it happens here a lot for babies or the mothers to die. Several of our children's mothers died when they gave birth. Usually they don't make it to a hospital like this woman did, but I do not know when she got here. They often live far away in villages and can't get to see a doctor, then most cannot afford the money for the hospital kit. It's money; it's transportation; it's poor medical care. All of it. You know, Franck's mother died giving birth to him. She saw him, said, 'Oh, my baby!' then immediately died. Same with Ahmadou's mother. In fact, she was dead in the bed with him and nobody knew she had died. That baby cried and cried and the dead mother could not answer."

"You know, Randy," Lillian commented after awhile, "I just heard some of the patients sitting on the bench outside the office talking about an execution in the streets here this week. Is that true?"

"Oh sure," he replied without hesitation, as if it were a daily occurrence.

"In the streets?" Nan asked.

"Yes, when people steal something or murder someone, we don't wait for the police to do something about it. We know they'll just accept a bribe and the person will get away. Instead, about a hundred people gather around the person, throw a tire over their neck and light it on fire. They make sure the person doesn't get away."

"But that's murder!" I exclaimed.

"Well, yes, but the person deserves it. They know that could happen when they do it," he responded sensibly.

"But don't the people get caught who do the killing?"

"How is anyone going to catch them? There's too many of them. You can't tell who actually did it," Randy said.

Lillian helped us turn to a safer subject. "Randy, what exactly is an amplifier? Sister Jane told me the children wanted one and I don't know what it is. It sounds like just some sort of sound system that's going to make noise louder."

"No, no. An amplifier's a DVD and CD player. The children really want one to play their music when they practice dancing."

"Oh, like a boom box."

"Yes, like that."

"How much does it cost?"

"Two hundred dollars."

"Well, it just so happens that I have exactly two hundred dollars in my pocket from a friend at home, so we'll have to find a date when we can go into town and shop," Lillian offered eagerly. At that, even though we were almost back to the Home, Randy wheeled the truck around, and we raced back into town to an electronics store. He knew exactly where the amplifier was and how much it cost. In less than five minutes, he had made the purchase with Lillian's cash and was back in the truck for our ride to the Home, with the large, colorful box loaded in the back bed. Sure enough, big yellow letters on the side of the turquoise box said "Amplifier."

We snaked our way back through the crowded streets of Bamenda, packed with people three deep on motorcycles as others milled around. After five minutes Lillian exclaimed, "Uh oh, here we go again."

"What?" I asked, concerned.

"That darned hill," she said with exasperation and a little fear. As we made our way back to the orphanage, up the beaten-earth road which was now as slick as ice from the rain, we bounced and slid all over it, much worse than before. Up and down, left and right.

Someone screamed. A precipitous drop off was suddenly my full view out the left-hand back window, leading straight down a cliff with no guard rail. I gripped Nan's hand next to me as we quickly spun back to the center of the road. Local villagers came streaming out of their homes to watch us try to get up the hill.

Slowly the truck made progress, and I breathed a sigh of relief as we made it past the drop-off. Then a large hill loomed to our left, and we slid into a ditch. One of the local men jumped between our truck and the hill; we were terrified he was going to get penned between the two. I shut my eyes in fear, even as I realized this was probably a regular community occurrence and the man knew exactly what he was doing. The truck tires spun and spun as the villagers looked on, the ruts becoming deeper.

At last we were upright, cresting the incline and finally zooming around the corner into the courtyard of the orphanage. Lillian gave me a swift kick in the shin and told me not to embarrass Randy by telling Sister Jane. One look at my face and she could have told something was wrong, but fortunately Sister Jane didn't see us arriving.

As the truck came to an abrupt stop, Randy nonchalantly pulled the amplifier box out of the back. Suddenly at least fifteen children swarmed around the truck, clapping and shouting. "We got it! We got it! We've got our amplifier!"

Word spread quickly and more children gathered, grabbing at the box as the older boys took it inside to assemble it. Their gaiety was a wonderful antidote to what we had just experienced, but the image of the drop-off and near disaster wouldn't leave me.

At dinner that night, I broached the subject of the unsafe hill with Sister Jane. What if a van load of children went careening off the precipice?

"Mama Lizzie, I have been to the government about this. It is their road. I have been and been and nothing. They will do nothing for us," she lamented, confirming what Randy had told us earlier.

I was emotionally exhausted by the day's revelations. The far-reaching discussion about the AIDS pandemic, the dead baby, the report of the murder, and another near disaster on the hill gave me too much to ponder.

Notes

1. Widow cleansing dates back centuries and is practiced in many African countries, including Cameroon. It permits a man from the widow's village or her husband's family to force her to have sex with him—ostensibly to allow her husband's spirit to roam free in the afterlife. It is rooted in the belief that a woman is haunted by spirits after her husband dies or that she is thought to be "disturbed" if she abstains from sex. Another traditional belief holds that a widow who has not been cleansed can cause the whole community to be haunted. In many instances a widow must undergo this appalling ritual before she can be inherited.

2. See Ezekiel Kalipeni, *HIV and AIDS in Africa: Beyond Epidemiology*, (Boston: Blackwell Publishing, Ltd., 2004), 221 ff.

CHAPTER 30

Maternal and Infant Mortality

I continued to ponder the fate of the young mother and her dead baby, the orphans whose mothers had died in childbirth, and the $80 kit the woman needed in order to give birth in a hospital. Clearly there was a problem with both maternal and infant mortality in Cameroon, but I needed to know more.

"Sister Jane, does your brother have a cell phone?" I asked.

"Oh yes. About half the people in Cameroon have them."

"Could I call him? I'd love to ask him about healthcare here and the situation for mothers and babies in particular."

"Sure, but we'll have to wait until he's back at home on the weekend," she replied. "We can't talk to him when he's in the bush." I was glad to know we'd be able to reach him at all.

When the day finally came, I found myself excited to speak with her brother, Dr. Shu Walter Che. After some introductions, we got down to business. I shared what we'd seen and he was, as expected, quite knowledgeable.

"First of all, Elizabeth, you need to know that here in Cameroon we only have one doctor for every 10,500 people. There are very few of us to go around. For that reason, most people see nurses instead," he explained.

"The man that took us around the hospital was a nurse," I shared, "but I assumed he was a doctor because of his white coat."

"Most likely, you didn't see a doctor. You probably would have just seen nurses. Now in terms of there being a lot of children at the Home whose mothers died in childbirth, that's a reality. One in six women die giving birth here, whereas in your country it's more like one in every 2,500. So you see, that's a significant difference."

"What causes such a high rate?" I asked, surprised.

"Well, malaria, anemia, and botched abortions are part of it," he said, "but the primary causes are infection and bleeding during pregnancy or delivery. Our infant and maternal mortality rates are among the highest in the world. Would you believe that in Cameroon a woman dies almost every hour from the complications of pregnancy or childbirth?

"And the mortality rates are much worse in rural areas like where I am now. That's why as difficult as it is to be out here in the bush, at least I know I'm making a difference. Many of the births in Cameroon are not attended by a doctor or midwife. If they were, the incidence of death would be much lower for both mother and child."

"So do a lot of the women give birth at home?"

"Yes, that or they go to what we call a traditional birth attendant. They go to one when they are in labor and the attendant gives them special herbs, that sort of thing. As you might guess, it's much less expensive than going to a hospital, so it really comes down to finances. For these attendants they pay very little money or they barter. Poverty is a significant factor in why so many women die. If they had adequate, trained care, there would be far fewer deaths. Also, if the women could go for prenatal care, they would be treated so as not to pass on the AIDS virus to their baby, so it's a vicious cycle."

I was beginning to see that it was a luxury for a woman to have access to a hospital, much less to buy the $80 birthing kit.

"Is the government doing anything about this?" I asked.

"They're beginning to. The Ministry of Health now has what they call a 'roadmap for care' to improve the survival rates. We have health districts and their goal is to equip them all with trained professionals and adequate materials. They're also trying to train the traditional attendants to spot dangerous situations so they can get the woman to safety. The problem is, still only about 10 percent of the district centers have adequate staffing and materials, and that's abysmally low."

"What about infant mortality?"

"That's very high here also, Elizabeth. The UN statistics say that almost 9 percent of the babies die. Many of those are born prematurely or have infections. Now the Bamenda Hospital near my sister's orphanage has a decent neonatal unit where they care for very sick babies, but most of them never make it there."

"Is the lack of adequate healthcare pretty much true across the board?"

"Oh yes. Did you know that the life expectancy here in my country is only fifty-one years due in large part to our poor healthcare system?"

"No . . . but now that you mention it, I haven't seen a lot of old people. They just don't seem to be around. I thought maybe they just stayed inside or something."

"Well, they're inside alright," he said with a morbid chuckle, "inside a pine box. You see, nearly half our population is below the age of fourteen. When that's the case, and you have as many orphans as we do, particularly now from AIDS, there aren't enough people to take care of them. So it all works together, against the children."

I asked him about birth control, as I had earlier with Sister Jane.

"Well, only about one-fourth of our population who is sexually active uses it," he replied.

"The nurse at the hospital mentioned to us that male sexual dominance is a factor in that."

"That's definitely part of it. The other part is lack of availability. They live too far from a place where they can obtain it and like everything else, it's also economic."

I couldn't imagine how someone would begin to address these layers of problems, but I offered him my contact information, in the event that he could use my support.

"I'll keep that in mind, Elizabeth, and I'll let you know."

"Wonderful," I said, as our troubling conversation came to a close.

CHAPTER 31

Pauline Mboma

"Mama Lizzie, I want you to meet Pauline," Sister Jane said, walking up to me one day. "She's seventeen years. My dear, this child has just come to us in the middle of the night. You should have seen her. Her dress was all torn and she had walked all the way here without any shoes. She has a story to tell. It is one of the worst I have heard, but there is a question. She wants to write it for you and send it to you by e-mail."

"Certainly Pauline. Do you like to write? Would it help you to write down what's happened to you?"

"Yes, yes," she answered, her head lowered. "It's been so awful. I don't want to talk about it right now. My teachers tell me I am a good writer, and I will also get them to help me. I want to tell you my story and the story of many orphans just like me."

As Pauline slowly walked back down the road that morning, I couldn't help wondering what had brought her here the night before. Yes, I would look forward to her e-mail. I wondered if I would ever receive it.

What follows is Pauline's poignant, but all-too-typical story, just as Sister Jane e-mailed it to me:

My names are Pauline Mboma. I am seventeen years old and became an orphan when I was seven. My father died when I was five years old and my mother died two years later. Before I met my uncle I was living with another aunt. Unfortunately for me, my aunt died two years later and sorrow, desperation and frustration became my new companions. From there I had to go live with my grandmother where I attended Primary Three and Four. I am of the Pinyin tribe.

During my stay with my grandmother, my uncle and his wife visited us during summer holidays and decided to take me along, claiming that they wanted to give me a better life, a life that could not be achieved in the village. They mentioned education and other advantages that life in a town could offer me. They also decided to take me with them because they needed house help and saw that the three of us living with my grandmother were all orphans. For some reason, they thought it wise in reducing my grandmother's burden, to inflict a lot of pain and suffering on me.

What an exploitative world! From the day I met the Mr. and Mrs. I met slavery. I attended Primary Five while staying with them but could not continue Primary Six because of the torments, insults, and beatings I received. I ran away from home to meet my grandmother where she showered me with all the love I would ever need. I attended Primary Six in the village with her, but unfortunately my aunt came back for me, probably because she missed her slave. But she presented a different picture before my grandmother. She came with apologies and promises that she would never lay a finger on me or throw any dirty insult my way. My grandmother was convinced and let me go. I felt so sad when I was living with my aunt, but I had no choice. I felt no grudge against my grandmother who was living from hand to mouth and simply wanted the best for me.

When I went back to live with my aunt, I think she was prepared for vengeance because her attitude this time was horrible. There was open discrimination and a set of rules and regulations I had to follow. I was not supposed to dish food from the pot for myself except when she offered me food, no matter how hungry I was. I had no right even to sit and talk with her children. I was virtually a loner. The insults that were rained on me could shatter your heart and spirit into pieces. This time my uncle personally sent me back to the village because I was considered to be an intruder and a home breaker! Me, just a desperate orphan!

Consequently I had to go back to the village to my grandmother's home where I started secondary school with the help and support of my grandfather whom the cold hands of death snatched away from me that same year. I felt devastated and depressed and saw the cruelty of life, but still I did not give up. Faced with this dilemma, my aunt from abroad asked me to go and see my other aunt, the cruel one, so that she could assist me in buying my school needs with money that my nice aunt sent.

The Mrs. pleaded that I stay with her; she said she really regretted grandfather's death. My second year in secondary school was really great because I saw a changed person who became a friend, mother and good companion to me. I was well-fed and treated as a member of the family this time. All these niceties were probably because of the money that my aunt sent her. Who knows?

The next year I was promoted to Form Three. This same year the devil of wickedness attacked my aunt. The beatings started again and were worse than before. Insults were rained on me and my family. I skipped meals because nobody was willing to give me food. I was being punished for the slightest mistake and had to do all the domestic chores. Every one of them! I had to keep everywhere spotlessly clean before going to school. In our campus, lectures begin at 7:30 a.m. but I always reached school an hour or two late. Even if I got to school I slept in class because of fatigue and I was psychologically disturbed.

On the 27th of January 2009 my vicious aunt met me in the market while I was buying sweets. I will never, ever forget that day. I bought and sold sweets in school to meet my daily needs. To my great dismay and to that of onlookers, my aunt jumped on me beating, kicking, and shouting at me all at the same time! She created a huge scene calling me all sorts of names like, 'poor desperate orphan' and 'thief.' Even worse, she called me 'prostitute' and told everybody in the market that I exchanged myself for sweets. Finally she dragged me home.

The next day she met me sweeping the parlor. She immediately seized the brooms from me and started hitting me mercilessly with them. Her reason was that I did not open the iron door while sweeping; then a few hours later she drove me out of the house. At that juncture I did not want to go to the village to stress up my grandmother. I also did not want to drop out of school so I went back and pleaded and she took me back.

The final stroke was on the 9th of February when she asked me to pay her phone bill and I did obediently. I had her balance with me. She was on the balcony and said that I should never enter her room no matter what. So I asked her where she kept her change but got no response from her. It was getting dark so I wanted to close the door. I asked her if it was okay if I closed the door. She still ignored me. Confused, I left the door open and went inside my room. She started screaming at the top of her voice that I was heady and deaf and should've closed the door. She got me well-beaten, pushed me out of the house and locked the door immediately! I was crying and begging for her to open the door but she refused, so I went next door to beg for a place to pass the night. The neighbor did not accept me in, but asked me to go back home because she believed my aunt would let me in.

When I reached home I saw that my aunt had switched off the lights. I knocked on the door but she did not open it. I had to return to the neighbors, pleading. This time the neighbors took me in; I spent the night with them and early the next morning I went back home to ask for forgiveness for a crime I did not commit. My aunt did not give an ear, instead she jumped on me and got me well-flocked. She beat me and beat me. She tore the dress I was wearing and confiscated the few that I had in my room. She only gave me my books and a few of the belongings I had in my possession. Worst of all she kept on reminding me that my parents had died of AIDS. In such moments I always feel like jumping in a river! In all of these tortures, my uncle did not intervene to defend me. I was stranded. While I was on the streets crying, a good, caring person directed me to the Good Shepherd Home.

Mother Lizzie, for the past sixteen years I have lived a life of misery, desperation, stress, sorrow, regret and above all I lived like a wanderer moving from place to place. But I finally have someone I can call 'Mother' in the person of Sister Jane Mankaa. I have brothers and sisters in the Good Shepherd Home who generously share with me. Mama has bought me new books, a uniform, school shoes, and I'm starting school first thing tomorrow morning after the holiday break. There is a place now I can call home and so I have put behind me all the sadness. This Home has given me unspeakable joy.

These are the torments that other orphans go through when they live with relatives. Here at the Good Shepherd Home I feel that I have a family. I have lasting joy that I never imagined existed in this world. I'm in a family of more than fifty children and we care deeply for each other. It's a great pleasure taking care of my younger brothers and sisters because they are wonderful children. How I wish this could happen to other orphans out there. There are so many!

Thank you Mother Lizzie for letting me share my story with you. It is not only my story, but the story of every suffering orphan child in this world. I know that my deceased parents are smiling, for I am a happy child once again.

CHAPTER 32

Dancing with a Chicken on Your Head

Mama Mary is the nurse who works with Che at the Good Shepherd Home Annex in Batibo. As we soon discovered, she is not only a skilled nurse, but a superb seamstress. Earlier in our stay she had taken my measurements, along with Lillian's and Nan's, to make each of us a traditional African outfit. Now she had arrived to share the gifts.

At her urging, Lillian, Nan, and I went to try on our new outfits, specially made for the big party that afternoon. The blue and yellow cloth, with African designs throughout, was beautiful. It seemed that hospitality at the Good Shepherd Home included delicious meals, comfortable living quarters, hours of storytelling, *and* beautiful handmade clothes. I was overwhelmed by the juxtaposition of this generosity, creativity, and hospitality alongside enormous poverty and suffering.

As we walked back into the sitting area, several of the Sisters were watching the movie, *Mother Teresa*, starring Olivia Hussey, on DVD. I hadn't seen it and couldn't think of a better place to do so. As the movie unfolded, the similarities between Mother Teresa and Sister Jane were illuminating. They were both as compassionate and loving as they were strong and determined. They both had a vision and concrete plan for helping the poorest of the poor with no thought to their own welfare or safety.

Before I could get too nostalgic, in walked our "Mother Teresa" . . . carefully balancing a chicken on a tray on her head, laughing and dancing. "Oh, we're gonna eat some meat tonight!" she exclaimed exuberantly. "All the children—mmm hmm! We're gonna eat some meat tonight!"

Continuing her balancing act, she danced out the door and up to the outdoor fire pit. Other chickens had been brought up in less dramatic fashion, and I could hear and smell popcorn popping. A full-scale barbecue was in the making, and the kids were off practicing their dance show.

In the midst of all the gaiety, it struck me that we would soon be departing down the hill and away from the children and Sisters. Sadness began to well up within me until I looked up and there was Sister Jane again—dancing, playing her African drums, and clapping in the courtyard. Her contagious joy filled my heart as I went back to my guest quarters to get ready for the party of all parties.

Lillian, Nan, and I chatted excitedly as we slipped into our African dresses and put on make-up for the first time since we'd arrived. Sister Jane's whistles when we walked out let us know that it was worth the extra effort.

As soon as we arrived in the courtyard, corks came out of wine bottles, huge bowls of popcorn appeared, and music blared out of Lydia's amplifier. First came the younger children—boys in red soccer uniforms and girls in light blue skirts and white T-shirts, doing identical movements in time to the music with lots of hip action. Then out came white pom-poms and more dancing; next came the excellent Good Shepherd Dancers.[1]

We were all clapping and swaying when a metal bowl was placed on the ground in front of the performers. Joseph the chaplain went up first, dancing in time to the music as he dropped coins into it. Sister Jane and Che took their turns, and then we went. All the children cheered because of the money they were receiving, but mostly because they could see how much fun we were all having.

Sister Jane then disappeared and returned, dancing with the now-cooked chicken on top of her head on the aluminum tray. She danced around the courtyard, in and out, as the children danced and clapped some more. With great ceremony she put the chicken down on a bench and pulled out a large knife to cut the rare treat. That was the signal for the children to get their metal bowls. They did, all at once, stumbling over one another pushing, talking, and laughing.

Then we filled our plates and went inside with some of the children following us. What a delicious meal we had. We ate until we couldn't eat anymore, as more children wandered in and out of the sitting area.

After dinner, Lillian, Nan and I prepared to offer the gifts we had brought from the U.S. to the children. "Here, you give them out," I said to my friends, handing them the bag of pencils we had brought as gifts for the children: a pack of twelve for each child with their full name in gold letters on each one.

They passed the large, clear plastic bag of pencils back to me. "No you give them to the children. You bought them," Nan insisted.

"No, Elizabeth, this is your thing. Now go on," continued Lillian.

We gathered outside in the courtyard for the presentation. With mounting excitement in the air from all quarters, I took the amplifier microphone in my hand and began to read aloud: "Vanessa, Mobiya, Emmanuel, Samira, Nafi, Cyrille, Edison, Confidence, Precious, Joy . . ." As each child came up, all three of us hugged them and told them how much we had enjoyed our time with them. "Clemence, Julia, John, Maximillian," I continued until each child's name had been called. The toddlers received age-appropriate gifts as well, so each child had something special.

"Okay, children, it's time to get ready for bed. Go on. Go say your prayers and get in bed," Sister Jane called, shooing them back down the road with her hands. I walked Nafi to the gate to tell him goodnight and his little arms went around my waist. I could feel his diaphragm shaking up and down and realized he was crying.

"Nafi, Nafi," I said, leaning down to him.

"Don't go," he cried.

"Nafi, I will miss you so much, but I must go back to America," I told him, thinking of my children and husband eagerly awaiting my return.

He continued to cry and hug me.

"Nafi, come on, let's go inside and talk to Mama Jane. Okay? Can you do that? Let's go inside," I asked tenderly, my eyes stinging with tears.

We walked in to find Sister Jane sitting on the couch. "This is a tough night," I said to her. "Do you think Mobiya could take Nafi to his room? I think he needs someone with him." Out of the corner of my eye I saw Mankaa, the Sister who cared primarily for the babies and younger children.

"Come on, Mankaa," I said, thankful she had come in. "Let's walk Nafi to his room."

I grabbed one of Nafi's hands in mine, as Mankaa took his other hand, and the three of us walked together into the cool, dark night. Nafi's hand felt very small in mine. He seemed so vulnerable and, of course, he was. He was a nine-year-old orphan in a poverty-stricken country. My heart was in my throat as I blinked back tears.

The depth of my feelings surprised me. As a priest I was used to being with people in deeply emotional situations. I had held people's hands as they died and had consoled the living. I had baptized brain-dead babies and later buried them. I had prayed with people before critical operations, not knowing if they would make it through. But this was different. I was not a "priest" in this situation; I was a person. Still, I knew the best thing to do was to move down the road, literally, before I was a puddle of tears.

As we walked into his room, the other children surrounded Nafi, hugging him, talking to him, telling him he would be fine. "Nafi, I'll see you in the morning. I'll see you then. Okay? I love you," I told him, clearly.

"I love you too," he answered feebly.

"And thank you, Mankaa," I remarked, grateful for her presence. She turned and smiled at me, nodding her head.

I walked out and up to my room, and let the tears roll down my cheeks.

Note

1. Three years later, aided by a Spanish non-profit organization and professional television crew, the children made a professional song and dance video called "Bright Stars of Good Shepherd." For purchasing information, go to *www.elizabethgeitz.com* and click on "I Am That Child."

CHAPTER 33

Saying Our Goodbyes

"I'm down for the count," I shared, as I walked into our guest quarters. Lillian and Nan were methodically packing for our journey home. I told them what had just transpired and sat on my bed. My brightly colored blanket with flowers looked like a welcome resting spot for me.

"I don't know," I lamented, shaking my head. "It can't be good for Nafi to feel like this. Maybe I shouldn't have spent as much time with him as I did."

"Elizabeth," Lillian responded sternly, "that's not true. Yes, you should have spent every moment with him you could. Think what you've given him and the memories he'll have forever."

"That's true, but maybe I've just shown him what he never had. Of course I hugged him whenever I saw him. Of course I looked at him proudly as he read his letter of greeting and played such a good game of soccer. Of course he knew he had someone special looking at him during his dance performance. Of course he enjoyed having someone take him shopping for clothes, but he's never had that in his life. What have I done?"

"You haven't done anything but love him," Nan answered. "You've just loved him."

"Come on, let's pack. You're going to be fine," Lillian offered, in her no-nonsense way. "I know it's hard, but you'll feel better tomorrow. Now come on."

With a heavy heart, I packed each item in my suitcase and carry-on bag, being careful to put the clay nativity set in a safe spot.

As I lay in bed that night, I prayed for Nafi and the millions of other AIDS orphans just like him in Africa who have no one like Mama Jane to love and care for them, feed and clothe them, fight their school battles for them, and take them to the doctor. I prayed for Sister Jane, who had enough love for all of her children and then some. It was time for me to let go and put all of these children and the Sisters in the hands of their Creator, who loves them like a mother and father, a sister and brother, who weeps when they weep, laughs when they laugh. I held each one up in prayer and threw in a few prayers for myself while I was at it. Then I fell into a restless sleep.

I expected to awaken the next day refreshed and feeling decidedly better; I didn't. Instead I felt conflicted. I was getting ready to leave one of the most alive places I had ever been. I didn't know when I would be back or how I was going to accomplish all that I wanted to do when I got home. I was very clear that it was time to return to my husband, Michael, and my children, Charlotte and Mike. But how could I ever share the depth of what I had experienced in Cameroon with the most important people in my life?

With these thoughts swirling, we walked back up the hard-packed dirt road that morning for our last meal at the Home. After big hugs from Sister Jane, we sat down to one more breakfast of pancakes with bananas and syrup.

As I walked into the warm sun after breakfast, I saw the van already loaded with our bags in back. I looked down the hill and here came the children. All of them were dressed up to see us off. I hoped Nafi would be alright today. I hoped he would be better.

He arrived in one of his new outfits, still with a sad face, his large, expressive eyes brimming with tears. I was upbeat. I had to be.

"Nafi, there you are. You look great. I'm going to miss you, you know that? I'm really going to miss you. But you know what? I can't wait to tell Charlotte and Mike about you. They can't wait to see all the pictures I took of you and hear all our stories," I gushed, the words tumbling out of me as I willed them to somehow make him feel better.

"Nafi, I want you to do well in school, okay? Mama Jane says you can do much better if you'll just study a little harder. Will you do that for me? And I promise to write. Okay?"

He nodded his head and snuggled up to me one last time.

"Come on, Nafi," offered Mobiya. "You're gonna be alright. Let's go play some soccer."

Turning to Sister Jane, I begged her to give Nafi extra attention for the next couple of weeks. She laughed and assured me, "Nafi will be fine. Don't worry."

"Mama Lizzie, the children want you to say a prayer before you leave. Is that alright?" I was just putting my foot inside the car, so I stopped.

Wrestling my own emotions into order, I prayed in a voice loud enough for all to hear: "Most gracious God in heaven, thank you, thank you, thank you—for Sister Jane, for the Good Shepherd Home, and for each and every child and Sister here. You know what is in our hearts. You know how hard it is for Lillian, Nan, and me to leave, but we do so knowing that we are leaving our dear ones, our loved ones, in your warm embrace. Protect them from all that would harm them, be with them as they farm their land, feed their rabbits and pigs, do their chores, and say their prayers. Be with them as they go to school and help them as they study. Thank you for giving them Sister Jane and all the Sisters whose love for them is unconditional. Our hearts are overflowing with love and gratitude and to you we give thanks and glory. Amen."

"Amen," the children all proclaimed loudly, in unison.

With that, they began singing a goodbye song for us, their little voices soaring into the cloudless blue skies. We climbed into the back seat of the van with Randy and Laurence in front; I turned around for one last wave and one more glimpse of Nafi. We bounced back down the dirt-packed hill, to the beat of the African music, sliding to the left and the right and back to the center again.

Joining the Journey

Would you like to help children like Mobiya, Clemence, and Nafi? Come join the journey by supporting:

1. **The Good Shepherd Home for Children in Cameroon**—Go to *www.goodshepherdhome.org* to donate. Your donation can fund one of the Home's many sustainable projects, health needs, food, school fees, or the building of a secondary boarding school for the Home's orphans and other children in Cameroon. You may also click on the appropriate button and donate to the Good Shepherd Home Medical School Trust Fund for children who are accepted into medical school. The doctor-patient ratio in Cameroon is 1:10,500. All children receiving grants will be required to practice medicine in Cameroon for a minimum of five years.

   The U.S. Good Shepherd Home Advisory Board will send your donation to the area of greatest need. To donate to one of the specific projects cited above, print the form provided online and mail it in. All donations to the Good Shepherd Home for Children in Cameroon should be made payable to The Community of St. John Baptist, a 501(c)(3) organization in Mendham, New Jersey, that administers funds to the Home. All contributions are tax deductible with 100 percent going to the Good Shepherd Home.

2. **Episcopal Relief and Development**—Go to *www.er-d.org* and click on "Our Programs" for an overview of their many African programs. Episcopal Relief and Development partners with the worldwide Anglican Church and local organizations around the world to save lives and transform communities. All programs work toward achieving the eight Millennium Development Goals (MDGs), which aim to cut extreme global poverty in half by 2015. ERD is an independent 501 (c)(3) organization, and 85 percent of donated funds go directly to program needs.

3. **The Peace Corps**—Looking for a way to spend a gap year? Volunteer for the Peace Corps in Africa. If you can't commit that much time, you can donate to Peace Corps projects in Africa by clicking on the project of your choice on their website at *www.peacecorp.gov*. In choosing your project, remember the work of Dambisa Moyo; it is aid to sustainable projects and microfinancing that makes a lasting difference.

4. **UNICEF**—Go to *www.unicef.org* to support African children at risk. Click on 'Info by Country' and type in the name of the country of your choice to see a list of current UNICEF projects. UNICEF focuses on child survival and development; basic education and gender equality; HIV/AIDS and children; child protection from violence, exploitation, and abuse; and policy advocacy and partnership. UNICEF is the acronym for the original United Nations International Children's Emergency Fund; 90.5 percent of funds raised go directly to programming.

   To make a designated donation to a specific country for one of the purposes above, call 1-800-FOR-KIDS or 1-800-367-5437. Your check or money order can be mailed to: U.S. Fund for UNICEF, 125 Maiden Lane, New York, NY 10038. Specific donation earmarks cannot be made online, only by telephone.

5. **Heifer International**—To contribute to one of Heifer International's many projects, go to *www.heifer.org* to learn about their organization and to receive guidance for your personal fundraising efforts. Heifer International gives animals to people in developing nations to help them become self-sustaining, and it hosts projects in specific countries. To donate to a specific country, call 1-800-422-0474. A list of current projects will be e-mailed to you and you can donate to the one in which you are most interested. You cannot donate to a particular country online, only by telephone, then by a personal check mailed to Heifer International, ATTN: Donor Services, P. O. Box 8058, Little Rock, AR 72203. Heifer International is a 501(c)(3) charitable organization, with 76 percent of funding going to the program, and 24 percent for support services.

6. **International Gay and Lesbian Human Rights Commission**—To learn more and/or donate to an organization that works for gay and lesbian rights in Africa, go to their website at *www.iglhrc.org*. HRC's Africa Program fights for an end to human rights violations based on sexual orientation, gender identity, and gender expression in Africa and provides support to the growing sexual rights movement in the region. Their "Donate Now" page will tell you where to send a check that you can earmark for their critical, ongoing work.

7. **The African Economy**—Contribute to the economy of Africa by vacationing there or embarking on a safari. Joe Prather, president of the African Professional Hunters Association, will be delighted to set you up with the best outfitter and guide in the country of your choice. The APHA works to ensure that African game and wildlife continues to be conserved in order to ultimately benefit the local people. You can contact Joe at *prather@AfricanPHA. org*. Note: Safaris can cost anywhere from $400 to $2,500 per day, depending on whether it is a photographic or hunting safari; the type of game hunted is also a factor. These figures are accurate at time of publication and are subject to change.

8. **World Orphan Week, the second Monday in February each year**—There are 143 million orphaned children living in the world today and as many as 100 million more children abandoned worldwide, living in substandard and dangerous conditions (UNICEF estimates). World Orphan Week is an excellent time to raise awareness about this crisis. Host a program in your community, highlighting information contained in this book. Show the video on the Good Shepherd Home website at *www. goodshepherdhome.org* or share about another orphanage with which you are connected.

9. **Cameroonian Women**—One out of six women die while giving birth in Cameroon. Remember the woman who came to Sister Jane desperately needing $80 for a kit to enable her to give birth in a hospital? Without this kit, women are denied admission. We've started an organization that assembles and distributes these kits. To make a donation for one or more, go to *www.good shepherdhome.org*.

10. **Cameroonian Infrastructure**—Remember the stories about the perilous hill leading to the orphanage? It will cost $32,000 to repair, grade, and gravel the road, with concrete retaining walls to make it safe for the children for many years to come. Donate to this specific cause on the Good Shepherd Home website at *www.goodshepherdhome.org.* As soon as sufficient funds are received, the road will be constructed.

Using this book as a resource, you may also plan one of the following activities in your community:

1. **Form a book group** in your church or community and read *I Am That Child* using the Reading Group Study Guide that follows. Supplement your discussions by having participants research Africa in general, or Cameroon or another country. Study African culture, get involved, make up your own ways to help, and be sure to share your stories at *www.elizabethgeitz.com.*

2. **Host a gathering** in your home to spread the word about the needs of AIDS orphans throughout Africa. Serve African food (recipes can be found on *www.elizabethgeitz.com*). Show the inspiring video of Sister Jane and the orphanage found on *www.goodshepherdhome.org.* Ask for donations or show your guests how to donate online.

3. **Sponsor a bicycle or motorcycle ride, or a walk, for Cameroon** and gather sponsors. You can involve a group of people in your community, and donate the funds to one of the many projects suggested here.

4. **Teach a yoga class, knitting class, cooking class**, or another one of your passions, and donate the proceeds to one of the above-named charities. Let your students know where their fees are going. Urge them to read *I Am That Child* and join the journey with you.

Reading Group Study Guide

Use the study guide below for four sessions, each of which corresponds to one part of the book. You may also select the questions that interest you the most for a single-session discussion of the book.

Invite friends from different faith traditions, or no faith tradition, to join you. Consider hosting a potluck meal before or after the final session, and welcome participants to make African food. Go to *www. elizabethgeitz.com* and click on "I Am That Child" for sample recipes.

Part I: The Road to Cameroon

1. Discuss the two quotations at the beginning of Part I, and their relation to this section of the book.

2. Discuss your understanding of the AIDS pandemic in Africa prior to reading *I Am That Child*.

3. When the three sojourners gather in the author's home prior to departure, they discover they all grew up in the southern part of the United States. What is their initial understanding of race relations? What is the impact of their childhood on their desire to travel to Africa?

4. Does your childhood offer any clues as to why you are passionate about the things that concern you most deeply? What are those concerns, and how do they relate to your upbringing?

5. What do the three women see on their eight-hour drive to the orphanage? What surprises you? What concerns you?

6. How would you have responded in a situation like the one the travelers encountered in Chapter Three? Discuss the role of fear in this section. How does it affect the travelers? The orphans? The nuns?

7. What is your response to the author's relationship with Nafi, especially as it develops in Chapter Seven?

8. What cultural differences leap out to you in these opening chapters?

9. What justice issues do you see emerging?

10. What teachings from your faith tradition come to mind in Part I?

Part II: Listening with the Ear of the Heart

1. "Listening with the Ear of the Heart" is one of the rules of St. Benedict, the sixth-century saint considered to be the founder of Western Christian monasticism. How do this section title and the quotes at the start of this section resonate with you?

2. Discuss the history of Sister Jane's family, as she shares it in Chapter Eight. What are the "strands of pain" she has woven together? What experiences most seem to affect her personality and work?

3. What parts of Chapter Nine, Mobiya Dibango's story, speak to you most powerfully? If you have lost a parent or loved one, or know someone who has, compare and contrast the experience to Mobiya's.

4. In Chapter Ten, the author shares her spiritual and personal reflections on what she has experienced thus far and begins to make more connections with her past. Has the book raised any questions for you, or reminded you of past experiences? What are they?

5. Discuss the treatment of homosexual people in Africa. How has this affected the AIDS pandemic and treatment of African AIDS orphans? How are attitudes toward homosexuals similar to or different from those in your country?

6. Do you agree with Father Joseph Ngijoe that the orphans are "the face of AIDS in Africa today"? If this is true, how does it affect your response to the crisis?

7. How did you respond to Clemence Kalla's story in Chapter Twelve? Discuss the common tendency to treat orphans like slaves within their own extended families. Does this surprise you? Why or why not?

8. In Chapter Thirteen, Sister Jane has to make a tough choice about caring for the pregnant young mother. What would you do in her situation?

9. Sister Jane is initially resistant to the use of condoms to prevent AIDS. What do you make of her stance? What does it suggest for efforts to combat AIDS in Africa?

10. Go to YouTube and type in "Cameroon bottle dance." End your session by doing the dance as a group.

Part III: Deepening Awareness

1. What are the different types of slavery discussed in the book, especially in Chapter Sixteen? What are the connections, similarities, and differences between them?

2. In Chapter Sixteen, the author discusses her relationship to the Reverend John Rankin, a conductor on the Underground Railroad. Has someone in your family tree inspired you, particularly to stand up for justice and liberation?

3. The author writes, "Sister Jane was wise to bring up the issue of people of African descent in America. If we were concerned about her and the orphaned and abandoned children of Africa, shouldn't we be equally engaged with people of African descent in our own country?" Whatever your racial background, how would you answer her question?

4. In Chapter Eighteen, the author overhears a lively political conversation between men in town. Which of their reflections was "news" to you? What would you have asked them, if you could sit down and talk more?

5. In Chapter Nineteen, Sister Jane offers her prayer for the Home and for all of Africa. Read the prayer again. What part most stirs your heart? Why?

6. The author takes Nafi for a shopping trip in Chapter Twenty. What are the ethical questions she struggles with? What would you have done?

7. What has been your personal experience with racism or with racial privilege? (For a thorough discussion of white privilege, along with helpful exercises, see Judy H. Katz, *White Awareness: Handbook for Anti-racism Training*, Oklahoma City: University of Oklahoma Press, 2003).

8. In Chapter Twenty-one, "Love and Electric Blankets," the author discusses her relationship with Anner, and inspires very different responses from Sister Jane and Lillian. How would you respond? What is your understanding of "white guilt"?

9. What is the significance of the motto of the Good Shepherd Home, "May We All Be One"?

10. In Chapter Twenty-three, Vanessa's story, the author reflects, "Yes, I am that child, too, I realized. I am Vanessa and Mobiya and Clemence and Carine and Nafi and each and every child here." Have you ever experienced solidarity like this? Is such relationship possible across such a vast divide?

11. Chapter Twenty-four describes a church service at the Home in vivid detail. Do you have any experience with worship like this? What would excite you? What would be more challenging?

12. What is your response to the choir director's request for money in Chapter Twenty-five? How would it feel to maintain a "mantra" like the one the author and her friends were advised to keep, and not to give directly to people who ask for money?

Part IV: Lives Intertwined

1. Part IV begins with the following quotation by an unknown author: "No love, no friendship can cross the path of our destiny without leaving some kind of mark on it forever." Have you found this to be true in your own life? Share your reflections.

2. Discuss specific issues that have led to the increasing number of orphans and abandoned children in Africa—polygamy, epilepsy, high maternal and infant mortality rates, lack of healthcare and transportation infrastructure. Which of these issues are you most passionate about addressing, or to which do you feel most connected? Why?

3. Discuss specific issues that have exacerbated the AIDS pandemic in Africa—criminalization of homosexuality, polygamy, male sexual dominance of women, lack of education, and lack of condom use. Which of these issues are you most passionate about addressing, or to which do you feel most connected? Why?

4. In Chapter Thirty-two, the Sisters and the orphans host a great feast and celebration. What is the relationship of feasting, gratitude, and suffering, as you have seen it in this book?

5. What have you learned from the orphans of the Good Shepherd Home?

6. What is the role of spirituality and faith in *I Am That Child*? How would the lives of the orphans, Sister Jane, and the travelers be different without it?

7. Discuss the author's relationships with Nafi and Sister Jane. How did they contribute to her transformation? Would you have done anything differently in her situation?

8. How might your life story impact your response to the many issues raised in *I Am That Child*? What might that response be?

Acknowledgments

My deep appreciation goes first of all to Sister Jane Mankaa, the children, Sisters, and staff of the Good Shepherd Home Orphanage, and to Sister Jane's never wavering behind-the-scene friends and family—Amabo Brown, Ngwa Evodia Nehgah, Sister Mary Anne Ngum, and Dr. Shu Walters Che. Your dedication and commitment to Sister Jane's vision are beyond compare. And to all the children who welcomed Lillian, Nan, and me with open arms, I hope this book gives you some sense of how your lives have impacted ours.

To Mobiya, Clemence, Carine, Nafi, Vanessa, Cyrille, and Pauline, your willingness to forthrightly share the painful stories of your lives with me will I hope give others a sense of the lives of all orphans in Africa. The hardships you have endured and survived fill me with hope for you as individuals and for your country.

My gratitude goes also to members of the Good Shepherd Home Board, Bamenda, Cameroon who are keeping the vision alive and to the Good Shepherd Home Advisory Board in the United States who are working in partnership with them.

Where to begin the well-deserved thanks to those who have enabled the Good Shepherd Home to become reality? Without each and every person who has donated their love, time, and money it could not exist.

To the many individual sponsors of the children who lovingly contribute each month to their care, you have and are making a significant difference in their lives. They pray for you every day and will never forget you. Neither will I.

To those who have made one-time donations for specific needs of the Home like the dormitory rooms, you have given these children the first beds of their own. To those who have provided start-up money for the Home's self-sufficiency projects, you have contributed to their sense that they can provide for themselves, giving them hope for a new tomorrow. To those who have contributed to the Food for Life and the Healthcare for Life Funds, you are literally giving life to these children; to the Medical School Trust Fund, your seed money will someday change the face of who is able to practice medicine in Cameroon. Such individual sponsors and donors are too numerous to name, but you know who you are. May you be enriched and blessed by your connection to the Good Shepherd Home.

Many foundations and churches have literally laid the foundation for the Good Shepherd Home, enabling Sister Jane's remarkable ministry to begin and continue. First and foremost my heartfelt thanks goes to the Community of St. John Baptist, Mendham, New Jersey, especially to Sister Mary Lynne Pfitzinger and Sister Barbara Jean Packer; and to the Abangoh Children's Project, Montclair, New Jersey; Ashia Cameroon, Switzerland; St. Bartholomew's Episcopal Church, Cherry Hill, New Jersey; Benedictine Sisters, Clyde, Missouri; Benedictine Sisters, Wisconsin; Calvary Episcopal Church, Summit, New Jersey; Chantal Biya Foundation, Cameroon; Church of the Redeemer, Morristown, New Jersey; Christian Women's Fellowship, Presbyterian Church, Cameroon; Conamara Foundation, California; Dale Family Foundation, Nashville, Tennessee; Episcopal Diocese of New Jersey, Trenton, New Jersey; Episcopal Diocese of Newark, Newark, New Jersey; First Baptist Church, Beloit, Wisconsin; Good Shepherd and St. John's Episcopal Church, Milford, Pennsylvania; Good Shepherd Lutheran Church, Florham Park, New Jersey; Grace Episcopal Church, Madison, New Jersey; Order of Port Royal, Germany; Our Lady of the Mississippi Abbey, Dubuque, Iowa; Mount St. Bernard Abbey, Leicestershire, England; Movement for Peace and Disarmament for Peace (MPDL), Spain; Northeast School, Montclair, New Jersey; Red Thread Productions, New York, New York; Roman Catholic women's groups, Cameroon; The Rosenberg Foundation, New York, New York; Sisters of the Community of Jesus, Cape Cod, Massachusetts; St. Andrew's Episcopal Church, New Providence, New Jersey; St. James' Church, Yardville, New Jersey; St. Peter's Episcopal Church, Essex Fells, New Jersey; Trinity Episcopal Church, Marshall, Michigan; and the World Day of Prayer USA Committee. The breadth and variety of organizations that have supported the Good Shepherd Home is encouraging.

It takes the input of many people to bring a book to fruition. Without the support of countless friends along the way, *I Am That Child* would be far less than it is. My deep appreciation to the readers who offered helpful comments at different stages of manuscript preparation—Lillian Bessonett, Deborah Brien, Chris Brdlik, Lillian Cochran, Nan Curtis, Michael Elf, Annie Harris, Peggy Hodgkins, Jane Mankaa, Ncheh Divine Ndikum, Diane Porter, Mary Ann Rhoads, Brenda Ruello, Sean Strub, Janine Vernon, and Wayne Yerkes.

Two book clubs road-tested one of the later drafts of *I Am that Child*; their insightful comments helped clarify the vision and message of the book. To the Third Sunday Book Club—Audrey Anderson, Diane Ciccone, Cecilia B. Hodges, Gail R. Johnson, Debra Jones-Peart, Tracy Eskeridge Joseph, Zandra Maffett, Elaine Walker Marsh and Constance White your critiques were invaluable. To my Milford Book Club—Ronnie Biondo, Rosann Kalish, Celeste O'Neil, Bernadette Schilling, Barbara Tarquinio, Denny Wagner, and Joan Waldman I thank you for your encouragement and honest feedback. To both groups, my deep appreciation for your willingness to engage an in-process book and in so doing to help shape the final product.

To Amy Ferris, Martha Frankel and Sam Portaro my thanks for your support and encouragement as fellow authors.

To James Weis, your creative ideas and desire for more descriptive information brought the original draft to a new level. Here's to Harp and Tru!

To Annie Flanders, your guidance and enthusiasm literally birthed this book into being. Your suggestions for additional material added greatly to the final product. Here's to our fruitful collaboration.

To my editor, Stephanie Spellers, I have no doubt that God sent you to significantly shape and mold this book and to walk with me on my journey of completing *I Am That Child*. To my sister priest and fellow Southerner, I am indeed grateful.

To Lillian Cochran and Nan Curtis, what a journey filled with memories to last a lifetime. I will never forget the special times we shared, both those chronicled in this book and those that are not. I love you both.

To the family of Anner Weakley, especially her two daughters, Shirley Weakley Keesee and Mattie Weakley Tanner, thank you for sharing your mother with me those many years ago. She transformed my life and helped me become the person I am today. I am gratefully in your debt.

To Annie Harris, words cannot express what you mean to me. Our numerous discussions of your life and the life of your family in South Carolina and in the Northeast racial issues opened my eyes to the painful truth of life for African Americans both in the 1950s and today. Your supportive, unconditional love has made my ministry possible and filled me with hope during the rough times. You are my guardian angel.

Last and never least, I thank my never-failing, always supportive husband Michael; you're the best! From my first book to this, my eighth, you've been there each step of the way offering encouragement, support, and editorial advice. And to my two children, Charlotte and Mike, who have once again shared me with my computer, I love you both with all my heart.